WHEELCHAIR FOR SALE

A Story of Hope

MARVIN SALLEE
WITH CANDACE POPE

WINEPRESS **WP** PUBLISHING

WinePress Publishing (PO Box 428, Enumclaw, WA 98022) functions only as book publisher. As such, the ultimate design, content, editorial accuracy, and views expressed or implied in this work are those of the author.

Unless otherwise noted, all Scriptures are taken from the Holy Bible, New International Version, Copyright © 1973, 1978, 1984 by the International Bible Society. Used by permission of Zondervan Publishing House. The "NIV" and "New International Version" trademarks are registered in the United States Patent and Trademark Office by International Bible Society.

ISBN 13: 978-1-57921-875-1
ISBN 10: 1-57921-875-X
Library of Congress Catalog Card Number: 2006930443

TABLE OF CONTENTS

FOREWORD

The pages of this book tell a wonderful story that will inspire the reader on two fronts. One, there is the marvelous account of a pastor's physical struggle and the healing hand of God. Two, there is the equally marvelous account of a congregation that experiences the transforming power of God and increases its impact upon the community. Both accounts are stories that need to be told.

I met Marvin Sallee nearly eight years ago when I was called to be a member of the staff of the American Baptist Churches of Ohio. During these years I have had the privilege of working with the leaders of the Vinton Baptist Church as they wrestled with a vibrant and growing ministry that demanded new and enlarged facilities, while at the same time caring for their pastor during his critical physical struggles. My relationship with Marvin and his family has deepened into an appreciation for and a friendship with the ministry that the Lord has provided through him as a humble servant of the church.

In little-known places, and with common, ordinary people, remarkable ministries that inspire and encourage the church take place. We should not be surprised—though we often are—by such accounts, because the history of the early church is filled with similar stories of the power of

God—Father, Son, and Holy Spirit—working in the midst of people learning to live by faith.

I pray that the Lord will continue to bless the ministry of Pastor Sallee and his family as they serve the wonderful people of the Vinton Baptist Church and as they together live as missional people in their ever-expanding southeast Ohio community.

DR. WAYNE M. PAULSEN
Minister of Congregational Development
American Baptist Churches of Ohio
June 2006

PREFACE

Have you ever lost hope? Have you ever been so discouraged that you felt as though you were caught in the middle of a long, dark, endless tunnel? For Christians, regardless of how difficult life gets, there is always hope as we look forward to eternity with God. Even so, there are times when we *feel* hopeless. My prayer is that you will be encouraged and that your hope will be renewed as you read this book.

Many times in the Scriptures we are told to encourage one another. Encouragers give hope. During the early years after my home church, Sunrise Baptist, ordained me to preach, I became discouraged at times about my lack of education and ability to be the kind of pastor God wanted me to be. But there were always people in the churches who encouraged me to keep on keeping on. Often, in the midst of my struggle, someone would say, "Marvin, you are going to make it." That gave me hope.

The *dis*couragers in my life have been few and far between, and in most cases their discouraging words only served to make me more determined to prove them wrong. When our four children were young, Ethel May and I were advised to prepare for the possibility that they wouldn't stay involved in the church as adults. This discourager was certain the kids would rebel against living the life of "pks" (preacher's kids). But God is faithful, and even though they sacrificed the "normal" life, all four married faithful Christians and are raising their children with the help of church family.

Soon after I sensed God's calling me to be a full-time pastor, I sought counsel from area church leaders. With only a high school education, a full-time job, and a young family, I must have appeared somewhat pathetic to those men as I asked for their help. They smiled, shook their heads, and said I should be satisfied to stay in one small church part time, since I would have to complete years of higher education before I could become an effective pastor. I was hurt and discouraged, but not hopeless for long, as I turned the matter over to God. Today I have a master's degree, and yes, I have learned much that has, no doubt, made me more effective as a leader and teacher. But it has always been God that made the difference in people's lives, not my formal education.

Things looked hopeless the day the doctor said my illness was terminal, that I probably had no more than seven months to live. When the people at Vinton Baptist Church (as well as those in many other churches) received this information, they refused to give up. They continued to pray, and their faithfulness fanned the dying embers of my hope. Together we kept on keeping on, believing God had a plan, growing in the various areas of ministry, serving others.

Everyone goes through difficult times in this life. I do not know who you are or what you may be going through, but I know the One who does. He is the God of hope. Don't give up, back down, or turn around. Press on, believe God, and finish the race strong. The Scriptures say that regardless of how things look here on earth, we are the ultimate winners. Jesus is Victor!

THANK YOU

To my bride of forty-four years, Ethel May, who helped me understand the words, "in sickness and in health." Her constant encouragement renewed my hope.

To my children and their spouses: Brian and Rachel, Debbie and Keith, Becky and Chet, Sarah and Eric, whose gifts of leadership have made the tough times easier.

To the churches God has given me the privilege to be a part of: Sunrise Baptist, Good Hope Baptist, the Marietta Baptist Parish (Newport, Deucher, and Lawrence Baptist churches), and Vinton Baptist Church, where the gracious people have allowed me to be their pastor for twenty-two years.

To Candace Pope, who has listened to my story and made it readable.

To the reader: May your hope in Christ be renewed. God is able to do immeasurably more than we ask or imagine (Ephesians 3:20)!

God bless,
Marvin L. Sallee

(And for this we labor and strive),
that we have put our hope in the living God,
who is the Savior of all men,
and especially of those who believe.
—1 Timothy 4:10

CHAPTER ONE

FOR SUCH A TIME AS THIS

O*h, Father God, I can't do this any longer. Surely it is time to give up.* This was my silent prayer as I made my way onto the platform for the worship service. In less than two years, a mysterious illness had taken me from a slight tremor of one hand to total confinement in an electric wheelchair. Now, on this Sunday morning, June 27, 2004, it took all the strength I had to push the button to move the chair forward. Little did I know this would be my last sermon from a wheelchair.

I was exhausted even before I left my house that morning. On Saturday I had suffered through many episodes of respiratory distress due to severe throat spasms, one of the symptoms of the unnamed disease. When the spasms hit, my vocal cords would close the upper end of my windpipe so that I could barely breathe in or out. A speech pathologist had taught me ways to relieve the spasms, but regardless of everything we tried, they continued to worsen.

By Saturday evening, after nearly losing consciousness several times throughout the afternoon, I had lost my resolve to continue preaching. I called Chet, an associate pastor, and gave him my outline for Sunday's sermon.

"Now, Marv, you'll feel better in the morning. I'll look at the outline, but you plan to give the sermon. Don't give up." I had heard those words from my family and my church family many times during the past months. For a long time I was, indeed, determined to not give in to the illness, to continue working full time as the senior pastor of Vinton Baptist Church. But during the past few weeks the thought that bothered me most wasn't so much whether or not I could endure the choking episodes, but how people in a worship service could possibly focus on God when it appeared I might drop dead at any moment.

The next morning, I took one more sip of water, guided the wheelchair toward the podium, squared up behind it, and pushed the button that brought me into a standing position. The straps around my waist and knees held me upright. I opened my Bible and began to read. As usual, the congregation was patient as I struggled through the verses. Normally, we aren't uncomfortable with silent pauses during worship; that's when we often "hear" from God, when hearts are moved. But on that Sunday morning, it was so obvious to everyone in the service that I was literally fighting for my life, and in the silence I could almost hear their prayers. They were suffering with me.

A few minutes into the message I signaled Chet and he picked up where I had left off. As he spoke, I backed the wheelchair away from the podium, lowered myself into the sitting position, and moved to the side. When I had recovered somewhat, Chet stepped away and allowed me to continue the sermon. However, a minute later, he picked it up again. Then, as I recovered, back to me. This happened

many times during that half hour, and later we were told it
looked as though we had planned it that way. Even though I
had only given Chet an outline, he had continued the message as though he had studied it in detail.

Finally, I gave the invitation. As the choir sang, people
moved from their seats to kneel at the altar. After allowing
for several minutes of quiet prayer, Chet stepped to the podium once again. "I think we need to pray for our pastor.
He's having a terrible time of it today."

Immediately, there were more than a hundred people surrounding me at the altar and on the platform. I was hardly
aware of the praying as I choked for air, but I did feel someone's hands on my ankles. It wasn't until days later that I
learned from John that he had sensed God's instruction to
take hold of my ankles while he prayed. He said he had been
praying desperately (as were many others) throughout that
sad and difficult service, "Lord, please help! Marv needs Your
help!"

"After you gave the invitation, I had a feeling that God was
telling me to go directly to you and pray. But I resisted and
stayed at my seat." John said he bargained with God, "OK,
Lord, if the music continues and Marvin stays there, I'll go."
Later, he laughed as he told me about the great sense of relief
that came over him when he finally obeyed God and hurried forward to pray. He had no idea why he immediately
grabbed hold of my ankles, but he held on as he heard Kent
and others around him "amen-ing" as he prayed aloud.

The service ended, and after many tearful hugs, my wife,
Ethel May, and I drove home. By mid-afternoon the throat
spasms had eased up and, although I had fallen while transferring from the wheelchair, I was feeling better. We decided
to go ahead with our plans to join our friends, Kevin and
Sandy, for a week of camping. They would leave Monday

morning with their large camper and get set up before we
arrived Monday afternoon.

Later Sunday evening, as I watched Ethel May pack our
bags, I said, "Honey, I've been thinking. If I fall more than
once the first night we're at the campground, let's come
home. There's no sense in ruining Kevin and Sandy's week.
OK?"

As usual, Ethel May smiled in agreement and continued
with the packing. She didn't say anything, but later she ad-
mitted she had thought, *Well, we'll be home on Tuesday.* After
all, for months I had been falling twenty to thirty times a day,
mostly in my efforts to transfer myself from bed to wheelchair, wheelchair to couch or chair, and vice versa. I hated
waking Ethel May or bothering anyone else, so I just had to
try it myself. Problem was, my attempts at being indepen-
dent usually ended with me lying flat on the floor, unable to
get up without help.

As so often happened in my life as a pastor, just as we were
about to leave the house early Monday afternoon, there was
a knock on the door. Ethel May and I exchanged the look
that said, "Well, we may as well forget about the trip."

I wheeled myself to the door, and there stood Scott, a
young man from the church, holding a fishing pole. "Well,
hello, Scott. Going fishing or already been?" There was a nice
fishing area in Raccoon Creek just a few hundred yards from
our house.

"I need to talk to you." The pained expression on Scott's
face prompted me to back up and invite him into the living
room. As I turned around to face him, he fell to the floor
in front of me and said, "Pastor, I don't deserve to be here.
I should have talked to you a long time ago, but today as I
was fishing, I had this feeling I had to come and see you right
away."

I tried to persuade him to get up and make himself comfortable in a chair, but he refused. Scott and his family had been struggling since the death of his younger brother. At the age of twenty-five, Jerrad had taken his own life, leaving the family devastated with grief. Scott wrestled with God for a long time after losing Jerrad, and he fought against diabolical forces that tried to convince him he was defeated, that he had no faith. Beaten down spiritually and emotionally, Scott had decided to fast and pray for God to give him strength. Looking up at me, he explained the fast had taken place more than a year ago and that he had included me in his prayers. Then something had happened.

"I didn't have a vision, but there was such a strong sense of God's presence and of His assurance that you would be whole again. As I finished praying, I sensed God saying I should tell you right away. But I didn't."

I started to speak, but Scott cried, "Pastor, I'm so sorry I didn't tell you about this months ago. I just didn't feel worthy after having so much trouble with my own faith. But out by the creek just now, I knew I had to come over here."

Putting my hand on his shoulder, I said, "Scott, don't feel bad about this. It may be that this is exactly the time God wanted you to tell me." After we talked a while, Scott headed back to the creek, and Ethel May and I finished loading the van.

At the campground, Ethel May drove as close to our assigned campsite as possible, and the lift and chair cooperated as I maneuvered myself onto the grassy area. After parking the van some distance away in the parking lot, Ethel May joined Kevin and Sandy as they opened the awning on the front of the camper. We needed it not only for shade, but also to protect the wheelchair, as it was much too heavy to lift into the camper.

It nearly killed me to sit there and watch while everyone else worked. I ached to be a contributor rather than a free-loader, so I slid out of the chair and actually crawled to help set up lawn chairs and put things where they needed to be.

After supper, we talked and enjoyed the coolness of the evening. Kevin's father had been ill for a long time, and his sister had called earlier to tell him they were transferring him to hospice care on Tuesday. Kevin and Sandy would return home early Tuesday morning, help with the arrangements for his dad, and be back at camp that evening. Ethel May and I assured them we would be fine.

Then came bedtime, time to formulate the game plan for getting me up and into the camper. Kevin would stand be-hind me, Sandy at my side, and Ethel May inside the door to pull me forward. I tried with all my strength to hold onto the sides of the door frame, but alas, my body plummeted back-ward into Kevin's arms. He kept me from hitting the ground, quickly set me upright, and after much struggling, the three of them got me inside the doorway.

"Let's get him to the couch." I didn't know whose breath-less voice uttered those words, but there was no way I was going to move from that hide-a-bed for the remainder of the night. After Kevin and Sandy said good night and closed the door to their bedroom, I quietly let Ethel May in on my thoughts. We had to find a graceful way to leave so that Kev-in and Sandy wouldn't be burdened all week with taking care of me. Kevin already had enough on his plate with his dad's illness, and even though I knew they wouldn't want us to leave, I couldn't bear the thought of wearing them out. Again, because of the wonderful relationship Ethel May and I have always had in our marriage, no discussion was neces-sary. She simply understood.

As we settled into bed, we agreed we wouldn't say any-thing to Kevin about our leaving until they returned Tuesday evening. I wanted to remain in the roll of pastor to him, to minister to him as he went home to talk with his family about plans for his dad's care. That would leave him and Sandy three days to relax after we left. The plan was set. Lights out.

It was after midnight before I finally fell asleep, but when I awoke at 3 a.m., it seemed I had only blinked. Suddenly I was wide-awake with a strange awareness that I didn't simply wake up on my own. Then God spoke, not out loud, but in such a way that in my mind and spirit I knew it was He. "Marvin, the time of your healing is at hand. . . ." A short pause, then, "for such a time as this." I lay there, staring into the darkness, waiting, listening for more. But there was no "PS" or "by the way . . ." I wanted Him to say more! I was immediately convinced the message was from God and that He meant what He said, but I wanted to hear more about it. What? How? When? Lord, what does this mean?

My first impulse was to awaken Ethel May, but before I could speak, the words, "Think on these things," came to my mind. Those are the words written by the apostle Paul to the Philippians: "whatever is pure, whatever is lovely, whatever is admirable—if anything is excellent or praiseworthy—think about such things" (4:8). It seemed God was telling me to stay quiet and ponder His message. After a minute or two, I turned over and went back to sleep.

Tuesday morning, Kevin and Sandy left after breakfast. As they drove away, I waved from the wheelchair and Ethel May pulled up a lawn chair beside me. "Marv, you seem a little stronger this morning." I absentmindedly answered her with, "Uh, huh," then, "Honey, I want to take a walk."

Now, understandably, her response could have been, "Are you *crazy*?" But instead, she smiled and said, "You want to do what?"

"I want to take a walk." Ethel May stood, reached out both hands, and said the same words she had said to me the day I told her God was calling me to preach: "Well, if that's what you want to do, then we'd better get at it." At that moment, I realized I had to *act* on what God had told me at 3 A.M. I had to *receive* the healing. Things were quiet between God and me now; no reminder from Him about what He had said earlier. I had to consciously remember what He had said and act on it.

Ethel May took hold of both my hands and pulled me to my feet. I hadn't told her about the 3 A.M. message from God. She moved to my side and took my hand. "Honey, where do you want to go?"

"Let's go around that camper next to ours." My feet were already pointed in that direction.

She glanced toward the neighboring camper. "That's a long way."

"Yes, but let's try." Slowly we made our way around the camper and back to our front steps.

"How'd I do?" The look on my wife's face was one of mild surprise. She was impressed.

"Well, you walked. It wasn't your normal walk, but you walked!" As I settled back into the wheelchair, I said, "What do you mean, not normal?"

"Well, you were a little flat-footed, like a duck, I guess." Oh, well. I did walk.

By that time, it was midmorning, and I still hadn't told Ethel May about the message of my healing. I suggested we go somewhere for lunch. Eating out has always been the time when we discuss serious matters, so it seemed to me we should go to a restaurant to talk.

As I operated the controls that lifted me and the wheelchair into the van, Ethel May asked where I wanted to go. "How about Chinese?" Now, Chinese food has never been my favorite, but my wife just grinned and shook her head as she drove out of the parking lot toward the local Chinese restaurant.

The scene I am about to describe seems as though it happened in slow motion. The food was served buffet-style, so Ethel May prepared both our plates, and we settled into our places at the table. Simultaneously, we picked up our utensils, unrolled them from the napkins, and as we picked up our forks, I said, "Honey, there's something I need to talk to you about." Very purposefully, we laid our forks on the table, and I began to describe what had happened earlier that morning.

We talked and cried and prayed and ate. I wasn't surprised by Ethel May's reaction to the news. She seemed fully confident that if God said it, it must be so. No doubt whatsoever.

I left the restaurant in the wheelchair. I wanted so much to walk out, but it was much easier to control the chair while sitting in it than by trying to push the buttons and walk along beside it. Ethel May climbed into the driver's seat as I maneuvered onto the lift and into the van.

At the campground, we drove the van past the parking lot to the campsite in order to unload the wheelchair. We had agreed on the way that it was much too expensive to leave it in the van, that it would be more responsible to keep it nearby. (Again, I have no doubt Ethel May fully believed I was healed, but she may have been humoring me in order to convince me to take it slowly.) As I parked the chair under the canopy by the camper, Ethel May shifted gears. "I'll take the van back to the parking lot."

"I'll go with you," I said, as I took a few duck-like steps toward her. She questioned the advisability of my doing that. "Marv, it's a long walk back, and it's uphill." I was already beside her in the passenger seat. We exchanged the usual knowing grin and headed for the parking lot. A minute later, Ethel May turned off the engine and reached for her purse. My feet were on the pavement before she opened her door.

As she came around to the passenger side, I reached for her hand. I cannot express what a joy that was! For the first time in two years, I was able to walk side by side with my wife, holding hands. We take so much for granted in this life, and holding hands seems like such a small thing. But at that moment, that small thing was a huge gift from God Himself.

In silence, we started up the grade toward the camper. I doubt either of us could have spoken even if we had wanted to. What an indescribable joy it was to simply walk those few steps hand in hand, to have the privilege of doing something neither of us thought we would ever be able to do again!

Halfway up the driveway, I stopped, put my arms around my wife, and kissed her. We stood there for several moments with our arms around each other, crying tears of joy. God's love and favor enveloped us. "Holy" is the only word I know that describes the time we stood there together. I will never forget that blessing.

Now, years later, I am still in jaw-dropping, eyes-blinking, head-shaking awe of God. What a God we serve! Why would this almighty, all-powerful, all-knowing God be concerned with an ordinary human being like me? Or for a little church tucked away in the hills of Ohio? Evidently, He had a plan.

> Praise the Lord, O my soul;
> all my inmost being, praise his holy name.
> Praise the Lord, O my soul,
> and forget not all his benefits—
> who forgives all your sins
> and heals all your diseases,
> who redeems your life from the pit

and crowns you with love and compassion,
who satisfies your desires with good things
so that your youth is renewed like the eagle's
—Psalm 103:1–5

CHAPTER TWO

HUMBLE BEGINNINGS

Please allow me to preface this chapter with a warning that you won't find anything very exciting in these next few pages. Thanks to modern media, we constantly expect to see and hear only exciting, hardly believable stories. But it is so important to remember that God works through ordinary people to accomplish His extraordinary will. Jesus wasn't looking for celebrities when, one by one, He chose the twelve apostles. They were just like many of us: common people who are experiencing an awesome God because we have given Him control of our lives. So please bear with me as I tell you a little about my family and the events that led me to Vinton Baptist Church.

My twin sister, Marlene, and I were born on August 13, 1942. On the very first Sunday after our birth, we were christened in our little church with Mom, Dad, and our older brothers, Clayton and Richard, looking on. My parents were faithful Christians, and though they didn't regard christening to be related to the salvation experience, they strongly believed in dedicating their children to God.

Within a few years after Marlene and I were born, there were two more babies who died shortly after birth. Then came Robert, Melinda, and then Paul. We lived on seven acres of land near Parkersburg, West Virginia, and every inch of it was used to provide food for our family. We kids picked berries and went door to door selling them along with Christmas cards and Cloverine salve. I had a daily morning and an evening paper route, and every week Robert and I stood by the road and sold Sunday papers. All our earnings always went straight to Mom and Dad. I wasn't good at making change, so people would often tell me to keep it. In that way, I suppose you could say my weakness in math proved profitable.

As kids, we were never aware of how poor we were. Mom would save all our earnings, and every August she used most of it to buy our school clothes. She was from a large family, also, so providing for so many people came naturally. Almost every day, we had fresh-baked bread and home-canned berries and vegetables. Housecleaning wasn't a priority for Mom, but it seemed she was always doing laundry. The clotheslines in the yard were always full and propped up with poles. I can still see the jeans and overalls flapping in the breeze. What a sight!

Both my grandfathers died before I knew them, but I have wonderful memories of my grandmothers. Grandma Sallee lived with us, and Grandma Powers lived nearby. Together they directed the making of apple butter every year. The women peeled apples, and the kids took turns stirring the huge kettles over the open fires in the back yard. Every year, Grandma Powers gave each of us a handkerchief and a pencil for Christmas.

My dad worked as a mechanic at a Chrysler dealership and later advanced to service manager. The highlight of our day came when it was almost time for him to come home from work. While Mom prepared supper, we would go down the road and watch for Dad's car to come into view. He would stop, wait for us to climb in, and take us back to the house. Suppertime was our time with Dad, and we never ate until he was home. After supper, he would watch the news on TV (that is, after we finally got a TV), then go outside to finish any work that needed to be done in the yard or around the house. Each evening before bedtime, Dad gave us instructions as to what we were to do the next day. To this day, I like to have a plan when I get up in the morning.

We never ate out, and we never stayed in a hotel, but each year Dad made sure we went somewhere for a few days to have fun. A day at Camden Park, a small amusement park a few hours from home, was a big trip. Eating canned beans from a picnic basket was a treat. Again, we kids didn't know we were poor, and we never felt deprived. Life was good, and we were taught to be thankful.

Dad loved to fish, and one day he took Robert and me fishing. Mom had packed each of us a sack lunch, and after Robert and I had probably done more goofing off than fishing, Dad said it was time to eat. We sat in the grass by the creek, reached into our little brown bags, and pulled out our sandwiches.

"Oh, Dad," I moaned, "Mom made me a cheese sandwich and I hate cheese!"

Dad looked me in the eye and said, "Well, son, you have to learn to be thankful for what you have." I ate the cheese sandwich.

Another lesson my parents taught us was in regard to tithing our income; that is, giving no less than ten percent to the Lord. Every Sunday morning there were seven stacks of coins lined up on the old upright piano, one stack for each child to take to Sunday school. As I look back, I am amazed that it was never just pennies. I don't know how Mom and Dad did it, but each stack was a significant amount of money, and we knew our giving was a serious matter and not simply a gesture. In this and in other spiritual areas, such as prayer and Bible study, my parents never preached to us. They simply demonstrated it with their day-to-day lives.

When I was ten years old, Dad accepted the call to preach. As a child, he had attended the Christian Church with his parents. When he married my mother, she was attending the United Brethren Church, so they continued there. They moved to another house when I was about a year old, and the nearby church was the Sunrise Baptist Church, so that's where we worshiped. Denomination was never an issue with my parents. They simply worshiped God.

Dad had held various offices in the church and eventually was ordained as a deacon. He grew spiritually in that office and even began to speak, but he had a slight stutter and didn't really think of himself as a speaker. Therefore, when he was called to preach, he questioned God's instructions. Eventually, he trusted God to deal with the stutter, and it disappeared. One other thing my dad felt he should deal with before becoming a pastor: he enjoyed King Edward cigars. Of course, God helped him with that, too. I still have one of his King Edward cigar boxes.

Neither of my parents went to college. Dad was a high school graduate, and Mom had quit school in the tenth grade to go to work. So, when he was called to preach, my dad took some classes at a local college. He never got a degree, but Sunrise Baptist Church licensed him to preach and later ordained him. The first church he pastored was called Ebenezer Baptist. It was located on a winding road far from our home. On a good day, it would take us more than an hour to get there, but when the creek was up, we had to walk part of the way. We always took boots and lanterns in the car, and on the days we had to walk, we formed a single line—Mom and Dad on the ends, seven kids in the middle—and made our way to the church building. Often we outnumbered the congregation, but the people there loved the Lord, and they had a great impact on my life.

My mother was a quiet person who demonstrated her faith in God in her day-to-day living. She had beautiful handwriting and was known for the thoughtful cards she often sent to others. Mom loved to read, which is probably where I got my love for reading. She also sang with the best alto voice I have ever heard. Dad played guitar and sang the lead and Mom harmonized. I learned to sing tenor by listening as they sang "In the Garden" and "I've Got a Mansion." My twin sister, Marlene, and I sang these songs together at school functions. In the beginning, I would sing the lead and Marlene the alto/tenor part. But later on, we battled for who would get to sing "Mom's part."

Marlene and I had very different personalities, but, perhaps because we were twins, we always enjoyed a very close friendship. Regardless of the distance between us, we could sense each other's emotional states and would often call to talk about whatever was on our minds. Until seventh grade, we were always in the same classroom for every class. When the teachers at the junior high school informed us we would not be allowed to stay in the same classroom, we were not happy campers! The separation continued, however, until we stood in line together at our high school graduation.

I still miss the days when the family would gather around the piano and sing for hours. Marlene was a gifted pianist. She also loved to read and often sent me books. Every year until she died, Marlene sent me a new Bible with a note written in the front. She was my cheerleader, and I was hers. She died suddenly at the age of fifty-five of a brain aneurysm. Although it was difficult, it was a privilege to preach her funeral, to have the opportunity to say how much she meant to me. I still miss my twin sister.

All four of my brothers and my younger sister, Melinda, are still alive and well, and we enjoy a close family relationship. Clayton, the oldest, was always eager to learn new things. He went to college and worked at Kresges (later named K Mart) washing dishes and serving at the soda fountain, then advanced to a management position. The local church was and still is a very important part of Clayton's life. I am not gifted in the area of carpentry, so I am in awe of those who have those skills. Clayton once built a new porch on his mother-in-law's home after simply watching and learning as a neighbor built a porch across the street.

Richard is also gifted at building and fixing things, and he is the family's go-to person for financial advice. Again, since by nature I seem to be foreign to math, I have great respect for those who are math-friendly. When our father was ill and dying, it was Richard who came alongside our stepmother to help her manage Dad's care and finances. (Our mother had passed away several years earlier.)

Next in line is Robert. Robert received Christ at an early age but later became sidetracked and ended up totally derailed for several years from living his life for God. However, he now has a strong faith, is a gifted musician, and loves to come alongside others in the church, helping them to stay on track for God. He is also licensed and ordained to preach.

Melinda, my younger sister, has come through some very difficult times. Her husband and fifty other men died at a power plant when a tower they were working on collapsed. Left alone with a toddler and an infant, Melinda remained single for several years, then remarried, divorced, and is now single and happily involved in her work and with her children and grandchildren. She is also a gifted musician and is a vital part of our ministry, as she plays the piano and keyboard at Vinton Baptist Church.

The youngest in the family, Paul, was the only child at home for several years after the rest of us grew up and moved on. Like Melinda and Robert, he also suffered a failed marriage, but is now happily married to a wonderful woman. Paul likes to fix up old cars. He and his wife share my love for camping, and when they visited Vinton Baptist Church the first Sunday after my healing, we vowed to go camping together sometime in the future. Their presence in our service that day meant more to me than I can express.

The Sallee household did somewhat resemble the old *Father Knows Best* television show, but we had our ups and downs. We struggled and made mistakes. Some of us turned away from God, and then came back to God. The important thing is, not only did our love for each other never waver, but God's love was always apparent.

My teen years were uneventful. I wasn't athletic, so rather than being involved in school activities, my time was occupied mainly by work and chores at home. I was extremely shy and, having learned a strong work ethic from my father, I remained introverted as I focused on work rather than social activities. My first girlfriend came along when I was sixteen, and for two years what I considered a serious relationship consisted of walking to church together, occasionally seeing a movie, and sitting in the front porch swing. One day, as we walked home from church, I asked her why she wouldn't sing in the choir with me. When she replied, "I'm just not into that stuff," I knew we wouldn't be a couple much longer.

It was a painful parting of the ways for both of us, but even at the tender age of eighteen I knew I had to trust God to match me up with a woman who *was* "into that stuff." For what seemed like a very long time, I remained dateless. Then, almost two years later, at a local church revival meeting in the spring of 1962, I saw "the one." She, along with my family and others, had been invited to sing. As soon as she began her solo, I knew I had to meet her. Funny thing is, Ethel May had grown up only a mile from our house, she was two years behind me in school and we rode the same school bus, but we had never actually met.

Through friends, I discovered Ethel May was a senior in high school and worked part time at the G.C. Murphy store. Several days a week, I discovered, I needed items from that store. Ethel May began stopping by Wilson's Grocery more often, and before long, we were going for drives in my dad's 1950 Plymouth station wagon. What style!

We were engaged on August 13 and married on September 1, 1962, at Ethel May's home church. My father and her pastor conducted the small ceremony. With the three hundred dollars I had borrowed for our rings and the honeymoon, we drove away in the 1953 DeSoto my brother, Clayton, had given me. The trip was a sight-seeing tour around the beautiful state of West Virginia. It was my dream to be a farmer, and I had heard of a nice Black Angus cattle farm located in the eastern panhandle. Ethel May was happy to go there and wherever else I wanted to go. After forty-three years, it is still that way.

My father and I had purchased some farmland, and since there was already a big farmhouse on the property, we agreed that would be a good place for Ethel May and me to begin our life together. Along with making that house our home, Ethel May also learned how to milk the three cows Dad and I hoped would be the beginning of a large herd. I continued to work at Wilson's Grocery, and soon we were expecting our first child.

Beverly was born on August 4, 1963, one month before her due date. She was beautiful, with dark hair and eyes like her mother. In fact, she looked exactly like Ethel May. The pregnancy had been uneventful, so the early labor was our first sign of trouble. In those days, fathers weren't allowed to be involved in labor and delivery. After many hours, the doctor finally came to the waiting room to tell me my daughter was born but would not live. Sixty-one minutes after her birth, Beverly was in heaven with God. Ethel May never saw her. The doctor wouldn't allow it.

At the funeral, I carried the tiny casket myself. Ethel May was too ill to leave the hospital. In our grief, we didn't think to take pictures, so Ethel May looks forward to the day when she will see our firstborn daughter for the first time. Beverly has always been very much a part of our lives, and our other four children know they have a sister in heaven.

After losing Beverly, we were very nervous about having another baby. Even after much prayer, we worried constantly during the months before our son, Brian, entered the world.

Ethel May's parents and I had taken up residence in the waiting room of the obstetrics department, and even though the nurses came out from the labor and delivery area often to say all was well, I continued to pace. When the doctor said the labor might last several more hours, Mom and Dad Edman decided to go home for a rest. It had begun to snow on our way to the hospital, and Ethel May's parents didn't drive much, so I had picked them up. I took them home and sat down at the kitchen table for a cup of coffee. A minute later, the phone rang, and I raced out the door and drove our old car as fast as it would take me back to the hospital. Problem was I had run out of the house without my mother- and father-in-law. Thankfully, they were quick to forgive me.

Back in the waiting room, I resumed my pacing. When the doctor opened the door to tell me I had a healthy son (and an exhausted wife), I literally jumped and ran through the halls of that hospital proclaiming the good news. I literally grabbed the arms of people in the hallway and told them they had to go see my son. Again, hospitals were different then, and mothers and babies stayed several days. Fathers weren't allowed near the babies, so I spent as much time as possible looking at Brian through the glass window of the nursery.

Waiting to hold my son nearly killed me. Finally, I could wait no more. I broke the rules. As Ethel May and Brian waited for the nurse to bring a wheelchair to take them to the car, I scooped Brian up from the bed and held him until the nurse hurried in and placed him back into his mother's arms. The sad expression on my face must have been what prompted that same nurse to hand him back to me after the elevator door closed. It was one of the happiest moments of my life.

Eleven months later Debbie was born, and several years later Becky, and then Sarah. Each baby was a new and awesome blessing from God. During the first three years of our marriage, I continued to work at Wilson's Grocery. This was the time before the mega-market, when almost every customer was an old friend. The store was a gathering place, with a wonderful sense of community and belonging. But, happy as I was at Wilson's, I would soon have to move on.

With a growing family it became necessary for me to make my first move "out into the world" to a higher paying job. From Wilson's I went to work at a large bakery where I was surrounded by noise, conveyor belts, and semi-trucks. For six years, I was just another employee who worked sometimes seven days a week, sometimes eighteen to twenty-four hours straight. Because of this schedule, I was rarely in church, and I ached to be with my wife and children on Sundays.

A large company in Marietta, Ohio was hiring, and as soon as I heard the news, I hurried to apply. The schedule there would allow me to spend Sundays with my family. But after only twenty-nine days on the job, I (along with many others) was laid off. The manager explained there had been a mix-up in hiring and that we should return the following week to reapply for our same positions. Somehow, this didn't sound right to me, so I submitted applications to several other companies.

My confidence soared when I was offered jobs at two of those companies. But, after my wife and I discussed the matter, we agreed I should try to get on at the DuPont plant. DuPont was the apple of the employment world's eye in our area, but I had applied there a few years earlier and was told they would *never* hire me. I never knew why.

But now, with newfound confidence, I walked into the personnel office of the DuPont plant and asked the secretary for an application form. When the director heard my voice, he looked up from his desk and said, "Marvin, I need to talk to you." I got the job and worked there for almost ten years in the production department. How strange that the same man who had previously refused to consider me for a job would then turn around and hire me on the spot!

My work schedule at DuPont allowed me much more freedom to attend church, so I gradually became involved with the work of committees and boards at Sunrise Baptist Church. I see now that this work was preparing me for the future.

> As a father has compassion on his children,
> so the Lord has compassion on those who fear him;
> for he knows how we are formed,
> he remembers that we are dust.
> As for man, his days are like grass,
> he flourishes like a flower of the field;
> the wind blows over it and it is gone,
> and its place remembers it no more.

But from everlasting to everlasting
the Lord's love is with those who fear him,
and his righteousness with their children's children—
with those who keep his covenant
and remember to obey his precepts.
The Lord has established his throne in heaven,
and his kingdom rules over all.
—Psalm 103:17–19

CHAPTER THREE

THE CALL TO
FOREIGN COUNTRY

After a time of serving on committees and boards at Sunrise Baptist Church, I was asked to pastor at a small church in the area, Good Hope Baptist. I had actually sensed the call to preach at a youth event some years earlier. I was fifteen, and it was an American Baptist West Virginia Youth Rally in Parkersburg, West Virginia. The speaker had my full attention that day as he said, "If you sense that God has called you to serve Him, come forward and proclaim it publicly." Even though I felt the nudge on that call, I hesitated. Then, he said, "If you don't feel that God is calling you right now, but that you will respond to Him if He calls you in the future, come forward." I finally made my way to the front of the auditorium, but I knew I should have gone after the first invitation.

Now at Good Hope Baptist Church, it seemed God was telling me it was time to act on that calling. For the next five years, I served as part-time pastor there and continued to work full time at DuPont. When I was asked to be the pastor for the Marietta Parish (which consisted of three small churches: Newport Baptist, Lawrence Baptist, and Deucher Baptist), I had been working at DuPont for almost ten years. After much consideration, Ethel May and I agreed it was time to leave there. This move appeared especially foolish to my co-workers, as I was at the point of moving upward into management. But we truly believed God wanted me to focus only on being a pastor, even though it would put a severe crunch on our finances.

For six years, we attended two Sunday morning services, one Sunday evening service, and three weekly Bible studies. The kids attended three Bible schools each summer, and as Brian and Debbie grew into their teens, they became involved with youth activities at all three churches.

It was a wonderful time for my family and me. We had close friends at all three churches. People were sensitive to our needs, and we visited often in each others' homes. Our children would occasionally awaken to a breakfast prepared by someone from our church family who had arrived during the night to stay while Ethel May and I went to the hospital or a home where someone needed the pastor.

One day our American Baptist Church area minister called. "Marvin, there's a church in Vinton, Ohio that needs a pastor." Without taking a breath, I said, "No, thanks." He ignored my response and went on to say he would like to submit my name to the search committee because things were going well at the three churches in the Marietta Parish, and perhaps I was ready to move on. Again, I said no.

"You mean you're not willing to ask God about it first? Am I hearing you correctly?" I closed my eyes and tightened my grip on the phone. "Well, since you put it that way. But I am certainly not interested in leaving here." The three little churches I loved so much were, indeed, doing well. They had grown both in numbers and in spiritual maturity. In fact, each congregation needed a full-time pastor, and I dreaded the day when I might be asked to stay at only one.

"OK, go ahead and tell their pulpit committee about me." Ethel May walked into the room just as I hung up the phone and we began what would be a long and agonizing discussion. Certainly we trusted God, but it wasn't as though we had asked Him to move us away from Newport! During the next few weeks, as we prayed for God's will, it slowly became apparent that He did, indeed, intend for us to move.

My wife and I prayed for God to make it clear to us whether or not He wanted us in Vinton. I have to admit, when it began to look as though He did, I had a pretty tough time resisting the urge to argue with Him.

There have been a few times in my life when it seemed God spoke to me almost audibly. But most of the time, His message or answer to prayer comes through as a deep-down, inner "knowing." Unexplainably, I know that I know that I know.

This was how it was when I knew God wanted me to come to Vinton Baptist Church. I absolutely did not want to leave the people in those three little churches of the Marietta Parish who loved my family and me. I hated the thought of leaving the community where I had happily spent six years of my life. But I was willing to obey God, no matter what.

The first time I drove into the tiny village of Vinton, Ohio, I thought, "Lord, You can't be serious. Please say I misunderstood You." Vinton didn't even have a traffic light! "Lord, I know Newport isn't exactly a large city, but Marietta and Parkersburg are nearby. What will our kids do *here*?" It didn't take long to find the church, because there were only two cross-streets.

As we turned off the main road, we could see the church building at the other end of the street. However, there was a funeral in progress next door, and the man standing in the middle of the street directing traffic assumed we were there for the funeral. As he approached the car, I rolled down my window and explained. He introduced himself, and we discovered he was a deacon in the church and a member of the pulpit committee.

As Herb had instructed us, Ethel May and I parked the car and waited inside the church until Jean, Herb's wife, talked with us and showed us around. Of course, we didn't know that day that God had already planned for Herb and Jean to be our neighbors and friends for the next twenty-two years (and counting).

Ethel May and I returned home that day with heavy hearts, knowing God wanted us in Vinton, but agonizing about leaving our home, our family, and our church family. It is a good thing God didn't reveal to us the difficulties that lay ahead. Yes, I had dedicated my life to serving Him, but had I known, I may very well have pulled a "Jonah." There were many times during the next several years that I wanted to run away!

After much praying and lots of tears, we laid out the plan. I would move into the house in Vinton, and Ethel May and the kids would stay home until the end of the school year. They would come to Vinton every weekend to be with me and to attend church on Sunday. This plan was especially disturbing to Debbie, our high school junior, and her boyfriend, since it would put quite a crimp in their dating routine. The fact is, no one in the Sallee family was happy about the plan, but we knew it had to be.

The church leaders had told me about the pain and difficulties they had endured since a beloved pastor had left a few years earlier. He had been "one of their own," a local person, born and raised in Vinton, and had married and settled there with his own young family. When he had announced his conviction that God was leading him to another community, it had been a crushing blow emotionally to the people of the church.

After that pastor left, the church had several interim pastors, and then hired a pastor full time. That had not worked out, with much trouble arising within a year after his arrival.

By the time I came on the scene, there was so much pain and so much fear of more pain, everyone was on guard. No one wanted to take a chance on getting too attached to the Sallee family. But I wasn't aware of how deep and severe the pain was until years later. The fact is, I wasn't transparent about my own pain, either.

My family and I had a very difficult time. Ethel May missed her friends. The kids had to adjust to new schools. Debbie and Becky had the most difficulty. Debbie and her boyfriend ended their relationship that summer when it became painfully apparent that things wouldn't work out by long distance. By the time she began her senior year at North Gallia High School near Vinton, she had decided her parents' decision to move had ruined her life. She made such an effort to fit in and to *not* be known as a "preacher's kid" that, by the end of the school year, she had been voted "Best All-Around Girl" and prom queen.

Becky had a very difficult time as she entered the junior high school, which was housed in modular units due to lack of space in the main buildings. It seemed this separation only made things worse. Becky had always struggled with insecurity and in finding her place, but through sixth grade at Newport Junior High School, her teachers had been understanding and helpful. However, at the new school, two teachers took an immediate disliking to her and did not hesitate to let her know how they felt. The entire school year was quite a struggle!

Sarah, on the other hand, did well at the elementary school. She was dealing with health issues that required some special attention at school, and the wonderful teachers and other staff at the school saw that she was well taken care of. Many of the teachers there were Christians, and several were members of Vinton Baptist Church. I cannot express how much we appreciated the care and support Sarah received from them.

One of the best things about our move was that the University of Rio Grande was only seven miles from our home. Brian completed four years there while living at home and working for the post office, which was just across the street from our house. It was a huge blessing for us financially.

Everyone at Vinton Baptist Church was gracious and helpful as we settled in, but the pain was evident. My thought was that perhaps God had brought me here to help heal the hurts, get the church back on its feet, then return to Newport. I can imagine God must have been smiling at me and saying, "Everything will be fine, Marvin. Just trust Me."

One thing that appealed to me about Vinton Baptist was the organizational structure. The church seemed very organized, with a very detailed constitution. I was soon to learn that structure can be good, but there must be a balance, and that balance must come from the Holy Spirit. The detailed constitution probably came about as an effort by the people to avoid more pain. They felt they needed protection.

The sides were set; the lines drawn in the sand. The church leadership had their plans for the church; I had mine, and as we now know, God had His. The congregation seemed fairly satisfied so long as I kept the sermons interesting and ended the services on time. Ethel May and I longed for our friends back home. There were certainly times of wonderful fellowship and fun with our new church family, but it would be years until close friendships were formed.

Only recently have I shared with others the fact that, for at least the first five years after coming to Vinton, I was ready with a letter of resignation almost every Monday. I was impatient to see God work, to see changes for the better in the church. It simply seemed to me that no one else was impatient for progress. On the other hand, I have no doubt there were at least a few people who would have welcomed that letter of resignation! But—I'll say it again—God evidently had a plan.

> Blessed is the man who perseveres under trial,
> because when he has stood the test,
> he will receive the crown of life
> that God has promised to those who love him.
> —James 1:12

> Praise be to the God and Father of our Lord Jesus Christ,
> the Father of compassion and the God of all comfort,
> who comforts us in all our troubles,
> so that we can comfort those in any trouble
> with the comfort we ourselves have received from God.
> —2 Corinthians 1:3–4

CHAPTER FOUR

THE GREAT FLOOD OF '97:
DISCOVERING OUR PURPOSE

Little by little, step by tiny step, God began to raise up leaders in the church. Together we began to make decisions based on God's authority, not ours. Committee and board meetings gradually became times of prayer and focusing on discovering God's plan rather than business-as-usual. The congregation wasn't growing so much in number, but we were definitely "growing up."

The Sallee family, however, was growing in number. Brian and Rachel were married in 1990, Becky and Chet in 1991, and Debbie and Keith in 1992. Sarah was still in high school. It was wonderful to have all our children nearby, and Ethel May and I especially loved Sunday afternoons, when everyone gathered at our house for dinner.

Late in 1992, our choir director approached Debbie and asked if she might be interested in directing the choir. Jean said she simply sensed it was time for a change and that, since Debbie had quite an extensive musical background, she seemed to be the person for the job. Debbie had had no thoughts of taking on such a position, as she and Keith had just been married a month earlier, and they were discussing plans to travel frequently on weekends.

Debbie was torn between taking on the responsibility of choir director and being the carefree newlywed. But she and

Keith prayed about it, and in January of 1993 she agreed to take over as Jean stepped aside. The services continued in the order indicated in the bulletin each week, with Debbie conducting the choir's singing and one of the deacons leading the congregation.

We also continued to host the traditional, twice-a-year, week-long revival meetings. A special speaker from outside our geographic area would preach every night, and we usually had contests such as "fill a pew night" to encourage greater attendance. These "revivals" rarely resulted in true, church-wide spiritual revival, but we did learn from the teaching of many of the speakers, and the fellowship was good.

Gradually, between 1994 and 1997, we became aware of little nudges from God toward taking our hands off the worship services and allowing the Holy Spirit to lead. Debbie continually sensed God saying, "Help them to see Me." Her response was, "Lord, who am I? I need to see You more clearly before I can help anyone else!" She became more serious about her own spiritual growth, spending more time in the Word and in prayer.

Little by little, we began to see the results of those prayers. The choir seemed to have new life. There were sparks of fresh interest in the services, with more nodding of heads, more "amens," and more people were lingering afterward to talk and pray together. Certainly God had been present in Vinton Baptist Church for many years, but it seemed we were becoming more sensitive to Him and to each other. Then came the flood.

Springtime always brings lots of rain to southern Ohio. The rain, along with melting snow from the higher elevations, usually means rapidly rising creeks and rivers. The one-hundred-year-old Vinton Baptist Church building sits directly on the bank of Raccoon Creek, a beautiful, winding stream, ninety-nine miles long, that eventually empties into the Ohio River. My house is just down the block from the church, so my back yard also joins the bank of the creek.

Several times during the years since moving to Vinton, we had kept a cautious eye on the water as it crept toward our back door. Many roads in our area become impassible after heavy rains, so on that chilly Saturday evening in March of 1997 Ethel May and I turned off the lights and went to bed wondering how many of our church family would be able to drive to the morning service.

Early Sunday morning there was a knock at my front door. "Pastor, can you help me get some things up from my basement? The water is already up to my ankles!" It was Herb from next door. We made some calls and throughout that morning neighbors and church members carried furniture and items needed in their business upstairs to the first floor of the McCoy Moore Funeral Home.

By the time we finished there and proceeded next door to the church building, there was almost two feet of water in the church basement. We immediately began to carry classroom and nursery furniture upstairs. All afternoon we were up and down the stairs, in and out of the water. Finally, someone realized the electricity was still on and hurried to flip the main switch. The water covered the wall outlets!

It hadn't occurred to me that, if there was water in Herb's basement and in the church basement, there must be water in my own basement. There was, of course, but it was almost dark when Ethel May and I trudged home, so we decided we would deal with it Monday morning. Keith and Debbie's home, thankfully, sat high and dry several miles away, and they invited us to stay with them for the night. But we assured them we would be fine.

Early Monday morning we discovered the water in our basement was almost six feet deep. A wall had collapsed, and the fuel oil tank had overturned and spilled. The smell of fuel oil filled the house, and not only because of the intensity of the fumes but also because of my allergies, we hurried to pack up and move to Keith and Debbie's house. We would stay there for a few days, and Sarah would stay with Chet and Becky.

By Tuesday it was apparent that many people in and around Vinton had been forced from their homes by the flood. The damage was extensive. As the water receded and the cleanup began, Mayor DeWitt began immediately working with the local, state, and federal government to obtain the help we would need to rebuild.

Along with other areas in southern Ohio, Vinton was officially declared a disaster area, so FEMA (Federal Emergency Management Agency) was soon to become a presence in our lives. The vice president of the United States, two US senators, and many other state and local government officials toured our tiny village to examine the damage. The press coverage, especially of the vice president, led to much of the support and donations we received from all over the United States.

We didn't have a local Red Cross chapter at that time, so the office in Huntington, West Virginia, sixty miles away, sent a nurse to help Mayor DeWitt set up a shelter in the elementary school. The two women worked day and night for six days, serving meals and providing personal items and a place to sleep for anyone whose home was flooded.

By the end of the week, we had shoveled the mud out of the church basement and had scrubbed and disinfected as much as possible. The women of the church had also taken everything out of our house that could be washed in an effort to get out the odor of fuel oil. However, so much more would have to be done before Sarah, Ethel May, and I could move back in, and there were so many other families in need that we decided to put our personal concerns on the back burner. Those few days we had planned to stay with Keith and Debbie would turn into several months.

As word of the disaster spread, groups of people came from all over Ohio and surrounding states to help rebuild homes. Building supplies and household items came in by the truckload. I was a member of the town council, and we worked with the mayor and others in the community to set up storage areas for the donations.

I was at a chaplains' meeting at the local hospital when I received a phone call from the church secretary. "Pastor, there are about a hundred people in the sanctuary. They've been having lunch at the school until today, but . . ." The Red Cross had had to close the shelter when school was called back into session. The group who had been staying at the school had grown larger as workers came in to help with the cleanup and repairs.

"Go get some deli meat and bread and whatever else you need to fix their lunch. Tell them we'll have a hot meal for them tomorrow." I suppose there are always some communication breakdowns, but we had understood that the Red Cross would provide meals for as long as needed. Suddenly, we were on our own.

By the time I returned to Vinton, people were leaving the church, heading back to their duties. "Thanks for lunch!" "See you tomorrow, Pastor!" No one complained. I talked with several men and told them to spread the word that we would be serving lunch every day to workers and anyone else who needed it. After they left, I hurried inside to make a phone call.

"Kathy, could you come to the church tomorrow and cook lunch for the flood workers?" Kathy Marcum was one of our many dependable women who always pitched in to cook and help with church activities. She didn't hesitate. "Sure, Pastor, I'll be there in the morning."

For the next sixteen weeks, Kathy directed her kitchen crew (she always had plenty of help) as they not only served lunch but also provided a warm atmosphere for people to rest and talk. Vinton Baptist Church was the go-to place for food, and we directed people to shelter and supplies. Other churches in our area helped tremendously, but we had become the "headquarters" of the rebuilding operations.

Kathy never knew ahead of time how many people would show up for lunch. Sometimes there were fifty, sometimes more than a hundred. As the work was completed, builders who had come from far away returned home, so gradually the numbers decreased. Several weeks into the work, a group of Mennonite men who had come from another area in Ohio approached me as we finished up with one of the damaged homes.

"Pastor Sallee, we would like to get started on your house today." Of course, I waved them off with, "No, no, no. That can wait." But they were determined, and soon our house was even better than before the flood. Ethel May and I will be forever grateful to those faithful workers.

The repairs and rebuilding in and around Vinton went on for many months. In the meantime, Vinton Baptist Church was undergoing a shift in the right direction.

> "The King will reply, 'I tell you the truth,
> whatever you did for one of the least of these
> brothers of mine, you did for me.'"
> —Matthew 25:40

> "Give, and it will be given to you. A good measure,
> pressed down, shaken together and running over,

will be poured into your lap.
For with the measure you use,
it will be measured to you."
—Luke 6:38

The Sallee family, L to R: Marvin, Paul, Marlene, Robert, Mom, Richard, Dad, Melinda, Clayton.

The early years: Ethel May and I with Brian, Debbie, Becky, and Sarah.

My home church, Sunrise Baptist, where I was saved, baptized, and later ordained as a minister.

Good Hope Baptist Church, where I served as full-time pastor while also working full-time at DuPont.

Newport (above), Lawrence (below), and Deucher (right-above) Baptist Churches, where I served for six wonderful years.

What a thrill it was to earn my Master of Divinity Degree from Eastern Baptist Theological Seminary.

Debbie, Ethel May, and Sarah posed with me after graduation at Eastern Seminary.

The 1997 flood devastated the village of Vinton. Some homes had water to the ceilings of the first floor.

The foot-bridge behind Vinton Baptist Church was covered with Raccoon Creek. Normally, the water flows twenty feet below the bridge.

Vinton volunteer firefighters worked long hours during and after the flood.

Then Vice President, Al Gore, along with many other local, state, and federal government officials, visited Vinton to assess the damage after the water receded.

Help arrived from all over the United States to rebuild homes in and around Vinton.

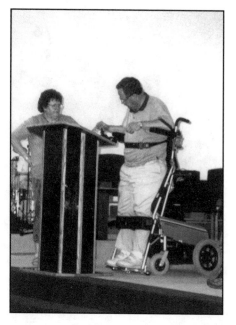

Ethel May helped me learn how to maneuver the fancy stand-up wheelchair around the platform. We had a few close calls as I sometimes rolled dangerously close to the steps!

This was taken after a wedding, as I returned from my office with the papers for the bride and groom to sign.

Praise and worship on the platform with the choir.

The gospel singing group, the Dove Brothers, honored me by allowing me to sing with them.

With the help of three Christian brothers, I finish the three-mile Jesus Walk at Easter time, 2004.

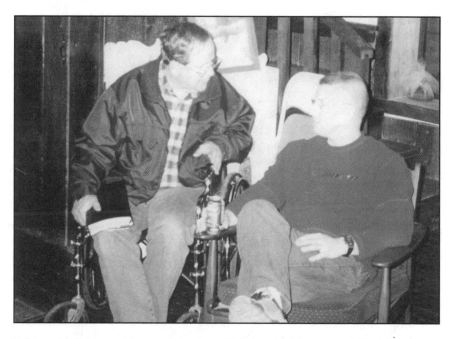

Talking with Jim in a cabin at a men's retreat. With the wheelchair, it would have been easier for all of us if I had stayed home. The many encouragers of Vinton Baptist and other churches kept me going. Certainly we can serve God regardless of our "wheelchairs."

Denver, Colorado, July 2005, after I received the Rosa O. Hall Award from the American Baptist Churches USA. L to R: the Rev. Dan Taylor and his wife, Rebecca; Ethel May and I; the Rev. Dr. Wayne Paulsen and his wife, Julie; the Rev. Dr. Lawrence Swain and his wife, Linda.

I had always wanted to see the Grand Canyon, and the trip to Colorado included a wonderful visit there for Ethel May and me.

Vinton Baptist Church buildings, past (above) and present (below).

CHAPTER FIVE

TURNING IN THE
RIGHT DIRECTION

I've been told an ocean liner travels over sixteen miles of water to turn around. By the late '90s, the SS Vinton Baptist was making its turn. If it had turned more quickly, as I had wanted during the earlier years, we would have capsized. God was not only teaching me patience, but He had also provided the time for me to take courses that would lead to my obtaining a bachelor's degree in Religious Education and eventually a Master of Divinity. I had come to Vinton as a high school graduate who had completed a few courses for college credit. I wanted more than anything to become the kind of pastor God wanted me to be, and I was continually enrolling in correspondence courses as well as driving many miles for classes.

When our kids were small, they would call out from the back seat of the car, "Are we there, yet?" I was like them as I asked God over and over, "When are we going to get there, Lord?" I was in a hurry to turn the ship, to get the degree, to raise up leaders in the church. But God is my awesome, patient Father who knew I needed to learn how to apply all that useful knowledge from all those classes. He knew I had as much (or more) to learn as everyone else in the church. God's classroom was (and is) a wonderful place to be!

By early 1998, Vinton Baptist Church was fairly well known as a "hospital for sinners" rather than a "showplace for saints." We were learning to be sensitive to the needs of those in the church family as well as to those outside the membership. Not only was the altar filled with prayers at both the middle-of-the-service prayer time and at invitation time, but many were staying long after services, praying and weeping, counseling and comforting.

All the growth and progress in the ministries of Vinton Baptist Church are a result of fervent prayer from those who desire to draw closer to God and to see His will accomplished. The church was growing with people who recognized the importance of prayer. The Intercessory Prayer Group met (and continues to meet) at the building on Monday evenings to pray for every aspect of the church, moving from room to room to pray specifically for the people and activities that would take place in each area.

Gradually, we moved from "doing church" well to experiencing true, heartfelt worship. Even choir practice went from an hour of singing to an hour of prayer and worship. Debbie began to share what the Lord was teaching her through quiet times and reading. At most practice times, the group formed a circle, clasped hands, and one by one each choir member would share a burden or need. As they prayed, they took the responsibility for petitioning God on behalf of each other's requests.

It didn't take long to notice how the choir had come to life. Debbie had become their worship leader rather than their director or conductor. She urged both the singers and the instrumentalists to realize their responsibility as worship leaders themselves. Together they would lead the congregation into a time of experiencing God's presence.

Slowly, Debbie and the choir introduced new songs and choruses of praise into the services. Spiritual growth became more apparent as we became more sensitive to individual needs and to God's awesome ability and willingness to enable us to serve Him by serving each other. We began to get a clearer picture of who we are compared to Him, and our focus became more and more vertical rather than horizontal. We were learning to fix our eyes on Him.

As attendance grew, we began to discuss the possibility of building an addition to the one-hundred-year-old structure. However, it didn't take long to realize that this was evidently not God's plan. Obviously, the building was in a floodplain, so this complicated everything in regard to insurance, building codes, and cost. As painful as it was for many who had attended church in this building for so many years, we had to face the fact that it was time to move if we intended to stay in step with God's plans for the ministry.

We organized a building committee and began the long and difficult task of finding property on which to build. Some in the group traveled to other churches to talk with their staff and examine the layout of their buildings. We wanted to learn as much as we could before finalizing any plans. Our prayers were for God's guidance in every aspect of the process.

In the meantime, God continued to turn the "ship." The more we focused on Him through the Bible and through prayer and praise, the more lives were changed. People were getting saved, marriages were healed, and many who had been ill were given a clean slate by their doctors. Sunday evening was usually "testimony time," and more and more people were standing to tell about the evidence of God in their lives.

Then, just when it seemed there was nothing but smooth sailing ahead, Ethel May and I suffered a family crisis that left us hurt and confused. In the months following this heartbreaking event, Ethel May and I struggled with the powers of darkness. We were more discouraged than ever before in our lives and even considered leaving the ministry. But with encouragement from our children and our church family, we stood firm on God's promises. Their love and support helped give us the strength we needed to deal with the pain.

Ethel May, in her role as a pastor's wife, had for a long time thought it necessary to keep her emotions under control and her burdens to herself. After all, she was the one who was supposed to minister to other women, not vice versa. But one day the dam broke, and she shared her heartache with a group of women who had gathered for prayer. This was a huge turning point for both my wife and for the women of the church.

As they put their arms around Ethel May and wept that day, a kind of healing took place that affected the entire church. We were all learning to be more transparent with each other and to trust in the love we shared as we grew closer to God Himself.

He died for us so that, whether we are awake or asleep,
we may live together with him.
Therefore encourage one another
and build each other up,
just as in fact you are doing.
—1 Thessalonians 5:10–11

CHAPTER SIX

DARK CLOUDS ON
THE HORIZON

As we planned for the new building, our prayer was, "Lord, what purposes do you have for us?" We wanted more than just a larger space in which to meet. We needed a structure that would facilitate the many ways in which we could minister to people in our area, a "hospital" rather than a "showplace."

The capital fund campaign was going very well. People were honoring their pledges and gave faithfully and generously toward the construction. At times, it was like Christmas at the building committee meetings as we each expressed our wishes. One of our top priorities was to have counseling rooms near the office area, which would provide for a much warmer atmosphere than the classrooms our trained biblical counselors had been using.

Both the children's and teen's ministries were exploding, so we needed more and larger classrooms. We also hoped to someday open a childcare center, so the nurseries, classrooms, and kitchen had to measure up to certain regulations. Then there was the fellowship hall, the sound system, the parking lot, storage areas, and a million details to attend to while staying within the projected budget. Step by step, prayer by prayer, God showed us the way.

In late autumn of 2001, I stubbornly ignored the fact that I have allergies, and I raked and burned leaves in my yard. Of course, this triggered the respiratory problems that usually cleared up within a few days. This time, however, I developed an infection in my lungs. By early 2002, I was taking several medications that didn't seem to be helping. One of my prescriptions was for large doses of Prednisone, a steroid prescribed to decrease the inflammation. It has many side effects, including interference with sleep, and even though I was exhausted from sleep deprivation, I continued to work.

In March I went to a large university hospital to see a doctor who specialized in lung diseases. He immediately decreased the steroid medication, and soon I was feeling better. As spring and warmer weather approached, I felt so much better, in fact, that Ethel May and I went shopping for a new camper.

We have always loved camping. The small camper we owned when the kids were young provided many wonderful memories (even though we were packed in like sardines!). But this new one would be our "dream camper," the one we would enjoy for the rest of our life together. We talked about all the places we wanted to visit, wondered where we should go first, and hoped our children and grandchildren would often enjoy traveling with us.

My twin sister, Marlene, had died suddenly in February that year when two aneurysms (defective blood vessels) in her brain had ruptured. When my right hand began to shake uncontrollably, my doctor thought it would be a good idea to make sure I didn't also have an aneurysm, especially considering we were twins.

After the CAT scan at our local hospital, he said, "Marvin, it looks like you do have a small aneurysm in your brain. I want you to go to a neurologist at the university hospital for some more tests." Of course, this was quite upsetting to my family, and right away our church family increased their praying.

It is our custom and practice at Vinton Baptist Church to anoint with oil anyone who needs healing. This is in agreement with the message in chapter five of the book of James. Of course, the anointing with oil James is talking about is the medical treatment they administered, so we consider our "anointing" to be symbolic of that. At the same time, we quietly gather around and pray in one accord for God to heal, if it is, indeed, His will. Of course, we also pray for doctors and other medical personnel and for the family.

Throughout the years we have experienced many healings as people have come together to pray for a Christian brother or sister who is ill and facing medical tests and procedures. Sometimes the healing takes place over time, but there have also been times when tests have shown cancer, for example, and after prayer, further testing proves there was none.

This was how it happened with me in regard to the aneurysm. The church prayed, we went on with our lives, and when the tests were done at the university hospital, there was no indication of a problem. The tremor, however, persisted.

Our first trip with the new vacation home was to Pigeon Forge, Tennessee. It was a wonderful week, but a dark cloud hovered overhead as my hand continued to shake. Little did we know that, after that trip, our new camper would remain in the driveway, unused, for the next two years.

> Your righteousness reaches to the skies, O God,
> you who have done great things.
> Who, O God, is like you?
> Though you have made me see troubles,
> many and bitter, you will restore my life again;

from the depths of the earth you will again bring me up.
You will increase my honor and comfort me once again.
                    —Psalm 71:19–21

CHAPTER SEVEN

STANDING FIRM

By the autumn of 2002 the tremor was worse. It was more severe when I was tired, and I hated that it might be a distraction during services. Often people in my church family would say, "Marv, are you OK? What does the doctor say is causing this?" My doctor wasn't sure of a diagnosis, but he had set up an appointment for me with another specialist at the university hospital in November.

Debbie went with me to that appointment. "Dad, are you sure you have your insurance card with you?" I pulled out my wallet and tried to get the card, but my hand wouldn't cooperate. As tears stung my eyes, Debbie put her hands on mine and said, "It's OK, Dad, we'll get it later." Then, with tears in her eyes, she asked, "Dad, are you scared?" I couldn't answer, but it was a question I didn't want to answer.

In the examination room, the doctor said, "Mr. Sallee, your symptoms indicate you have Parkinson's disease." The symptoms the doctor referred to included a shuffling stride and losing my balance and falling. In January 2003, I saw yet another doctor who informed us that we were dealing with a more severe kind of Parkinson's disease than they had previously thought. He said I probably had only a few months to live and that I should immediately get a wheelchair and try to make the most of the time I had left.

Neither my family nor the church was ready to accept such a grim prognosis. I continued to preach, and the prayers continued to flow. For a while, I was able to walk with help, but on the days I couldn't manage the fifty yards from my house to the church, I reluctantly used a wheelchair.

The old building was anything but handicap accessible, so the men would take their positions and lift me and the chair up the stairs and into the sanctuary. Then, they would help me up the two steps to the platform and onto the stool behind the pulpit. I was determined to continue as their pastor, and they were determined to help me do just that.

As much as I hated being dependent, I learned to appreciate the offers of help. Even when I protested, someone would insist, "Marv, we'll walk over to the house with you," or, "Pastor, stay right there. I'll get it for you," when I needed something out of my reach. There were always people behind and beside me to keep me from falling.

At home, Ethel May did her best to keep things as normal as possible. When it became dangerous for her to help me upstairs, we agreed it was time to move our bedroom into my first-floor study. I didn't mind so much giving up the study, but it was very painful when we had to pack away many of the knickknacks that reminded me of my parents and grandparents. Yes, they were only "things," but it was like giving up a part of me, part of my identity.

I continued to try to move around the house without help. After all, Ethel May had enough to do without waiting on me constantly. Of course, she preferred that I call for her, because on my worst days, she had to help me up from the floor many times after I had tried to make it from one room to another.

Amazingly, I never broke a bone as my body pitched backwards or to the side.

Often after I landed on the floor, my two-year-old grandson would run to Ethel May and say, "Uh-oh, Papaw, uh-oh!" Then he would run back to me and try to help me up.

In the meantime, the men and women of the church were working diligently on the new building. Early in the construction, I had been able to help, but by the time it was almost finished, all I could do was watch from the wheelchair. One of my most painful memories is of wheeling myself into the sanctuary and looking up toward the baptistery thinking, "I'll never be there. I won't be able to baptize anyone ever again."

It had been several months since I had been given the "death sentence" from the specialist, and I had been following up with my local doctor. Together we decided the terminal prognosis may have been a mistake, as I wasn't developing the expected symptoms of the disease. However, I had begun to have severe spasms of my vocal cords. When this happened, my trachea would constrict, leaving me struggling to breathe.

When Ethel May and the rest of the family compared notes, they concluded that the "asthma attacks" of the past months had probably been these spasms rather than something brought on by allergies. In the middle of a sermon, I would feel an attack coming on and would simply stop until it passed. God brought (and still brings) some very loving and patient people to Vinton Baptist Church!

Once, on the way home from a doctor's appointment at the university hospital, I had a severe attack. Debbie was driving, and even though she and Ethel May wanted to stop at a hospital along the way, I insisted I would be fine and that we should go home. When we arrived, my son-in-law, Keith, who is a registered nurse, took one look at me, and before I knew it I was in the emergency room of the local hospital. They hurried to send me back to the university hospital where I saw yet another doctor and received yet another diagnosis.

The frustration of not really knowing what we were dealing with was almost as stressful as the illness itself. Then, as more symptoms cropped up, the doctors were all but throwing up their hands. Next came painful muscle spasms in my head, of all things! I would be caught in mid-sentence as a vice clamped across my forehead. More and more often the sermon was put on pause as we waited for the throat spasms and/or the head spasms to pass. Prayers continued to flow heavenward.

One Sunday evening I had grown weary of sitting behind the pulpit. After the men had helped me to a regular chair on the main floor near the front pews, I finished the message, and we bowed for prayer. It was at this time, I later discovered, that one of our young men had a vision.

Rich was sitting at the end of a pew on the center aisle, head bowed, eyes closed. He was near the door, so he wasn't surprised by the soft rush of cool air that came from that direction as he prayed. But right away he had a sense that someone had come into the room. Without opening his eyes, he felt something brush his arm, then "saw" an angel move toward me at the front. The angel moved into the chair and held me on his lap with his arms around me. Then Rich "heard" him say, "I know all of you want Marvin healed right now, but this isn't about what you want. He is in my arms, under my care and control, and I'll take care of him in my time." Rich didn't hear an audible voice, but as the prayer ended and he opened his eyes, he knew he had experienced something awesome.

Not until a week later did Rich tell me about the vision. He told his wife on their way home, but as he explained, he wasn't sure he should say anything, as he was a little "freaked out." He had never experienced anything like this before. He talked to his father-in-law, Kevin, about it, and together they agreed I should know what had happened. I reacted calmly to the story. I certainly believed God had blessed Rich with the vision, and I had that peace of God that passes all understanding. But it would be almost two years before we were reminded of the message the angel gave to Rich that Sunday evening.

We moved into the new building in August of 2003. At that time, I was still using the manual wheelchair, coming onto the platform from the side door and down the ramp toward the podium. Funny thing, when we had begun to make plans for the new structure, we had discussed at length the importance of providing a ramp onto the platform for future choir members who might be in wheelchairs. It hadn't occurred to us then that the first wheelchair on the ramp would be mine!

For a while I was helped onto a stool at the podium as we had been accustomed to doing at the old building. But I hated sitting down to preach! I like to move around a lot as I speak, and even though I knew that wouldn't be possible, I at least wanted to be standing somehow.

Soon I was trying out a remarkable apparatus, a wheelchair that would stand me up with the push of a button! I had to be strapped around the waist and across both legs, but this amazing machine afforded me more mobility than I had had in a long time. One of our wonderful ladies even started on the project of altering my suits so that the straps wouldn't show!

Ethel May and I bought a van and had it equipped with a remote control wheelchair lift. The only problem was that I couldn't stay in the wheelchair to drive, so I had to transfer myself into the driver's seat from behind. Most of the time this was not a problem, but occasionally I would fall between the seats. More than once the church's secretary or the custodian would see my van parked just outside the front door and come out to find me trapped between the seats and unable to move. Of course, I would be lovingly reprimanded at those times for not notifying them that I was on my way to the church.

Week after week we experienced God's presence in the services as we continued to focus on Him. The new facility provided a larger and more comfortable place to meet, but the hearts of the people made it a place of worship. We were determined to stand firm against Satan and his attempts to break us down. God was, is, and always will be in control.

I believe this "standing firm" had a great deal to do with the drawing of new people to our worship services. Maybe a few came to see the "preacher in the stand-up wheelchair," but most came to see God. Hurting people flocked to the altar every Sunday to lay their burdens before the throne of God, to be prayed for by others, and to receive healing both for their bodies and for their souls.

Faithful believers continued to pray for my healing. Even though it was obvious my physical health was deteriorating, they never stopped praying. "Marv, I don't understand it, but I am not yet convinced it is God's will that you stay in that wheelchair. So, I'm going to keep praying for your complete healing until He tells me otherwise." These statements were more or less echoed throughout the congregation. If anyone had given up on me or on God, I didn't know about it.

Early in 2004, I met with Traci, a speech and language pathologist, to learn how to control the vocal cord spasms. The diagnosis she had received from my doctor was "paradoxical vocal cord dysfunction," so she set about teaching me ways to relieve the spasms, things which had helped others with this condition. But after many weeks of practicing the breathing exercises and the swallowing techniques, not only was there no improvement, but the spasms were stronger and more frequent.

Finally, as a last-ditch effort, Traci and my doctor agreed an injection of Botox might help. (This is the stuff plastic surgeons inject into faces to paralyze the muscles to reduce wrinkling.) So, back to the university hospital I went, where the doctor inserted a tube into my throat and paralyzed the muscles around the vocal cords. We saw no improvement after three of these treatments, so the doctor advised me to continue working with Traci.

Poor Traci! Her kindness and compassion must have masked her frustration as I continued a downhill slide. In her words: "Marvin worked so hard, but there were moments when it was a nightmare. As his throat closed, he would turn blood red. I remember at least three times I thought he would pass out, which actually would have helped, because the muscles would have relaxed and allowed him to breathe. But he never lost consciousness, and eventually he was able to get air into his lungs again."

Like the doctors, Traci was baffled. The symptoms didn't match the diagnosis. But no one wanted to give up on me, so I continued the therapy.

Nothing helped, and finally came that horrible Sunday when it was obvious I wouldn't be able to continue to function as a pastor. Then Monday, when I realized my camping days were also over. But God knew better. He knew that when the sun came up on Tuesday I would be thinking differently. He knew the joy and gratitude I would experience that day as I walked hand in hand with my wife up a grassy hillside.

> When I said, "My foot is slipping,"
> your love, O Lord, supported me.

When anxiety was great within me,
your consolation brought joy to my soul.
—Psalm 94:18–19

But as for me, I will always have hope;
I will praise you more and more.
My mouth will tell of your righteousness,
of your salvation all day long,
though I know not its measure.
—Psalm 71:14–15

CHAPTER EIGHT

TIME TO CELEBRATE

The short walk from the van to the campsite was a taste of heaven. By the time Ethel May and I reached the camper, it was mid-afternoon. "Marv, do you want to lie down for a while?" Wishful thinking!

"No, but you go ahead and take a nap. I think I'll sit here in the lawn chair and read." I picked up the book I'd been reading, but there was no way I was going to be able to concentrate on it. I peeked inside the camper, and Ethel May had already dozed off. I just had to walk!

I was having the time of my life, strolling up and down the narrow roadways between camp lots, circling, greeting other campers. By the time I reached the most distant corner of the campground, Ethel May had awakened and was searching for me. Finally, she spotted me in the distance and watched as I duck-footed my way along the road. I didn't see her until I rounded the corner. There she stood in the middle of the road, hands on her hips as if to say, "What in the world are you doing?"

As we met, she very sweetly asked, "Honey, what are you doing?" I'm sure I didn't need to answer that question, but I said, "Honey, I'm walking!" Once again we celebrated with a hug and held hands as we strolled back to our campsite. "Well, Marv, what now? Kevin and Sandy will be back this evening, but shouldn't we call the girls first and tell them about this?"

I was very concerned about the sensation this healing was going to generate among my church family and friends. I didn't want it to be blown into a "big show." After all, Jesus healed quietly. There were times when there were crowds already gathered around Him, but still He didn't make it into a huge performance or draw more attention to the situation by shouting, hitting, or waving His arms in the air. People were simply healed by His touch, His power.

Of course, neither did I want to keep this miracle a secret. The prayers of so many people had just been answered! God had been glorified in the illness, and now it was time to glorify Him in the healing. Ethel May and I agreed we would just have to leave it all to God. (What a novel idea!) He could handle the whole situation, and He would show us how to proceed.

I picked up the cell phone and dialed Debbie's number at work. "Dad? What's wrong?" I knew the call would scare her, especially after I had asked the operator to call her out of a meeting. "Nothing's wrong. Something has happened that I want to tell you about." There was silence as I told the story. "Debbie, are you there?"

"Oh, Dad, this is wonderful! How do you feel? Does it hurt to walk? Do you still have the tremor?" I was so thrilled to be walking, I hadn't thought about the tremor of my right hand. "Yes, my hand still shakes, but it seems like it is less than it was yesterday. Otherwise, my legs are a little stiff, but I feel fine."

Debbie called back a few minutes later to say she had reached Becky and Sarah with the news and that none of them would be able to get away to come to the campgrounds right away. "Debbie, I don't want all of you to rush down here. I don't want everyone to know about it, yet. I think it just needs to soak in for a while."

We decided together that all three daughters, their husbands and children, would come together after work on Wednesday. But Debbie continued to call almost every hour for a "progress report." By that evening, I was able to tell her that not only was I still walking, but the tremor was almost gone.

It was nearly dark when Kevin and Sandy returned. Ethel May and I were relaxing in the lawn chairs under the canopy, and we stayed there as they sat down and began to tell us about their day. We talked about the difficulties and the sadness we experience when our parents become elderly and in poor health. After a long while, Sandy asked what we had been doing all day.

Later, Kevin told us his heart sank to his feet when he saw me glance toward Ethel May as I said, "Well, there's something we want to talk to you about." He was sure I was about to say it was time to give up, to resign. But soon he had his hands in the air, praising God. We were all laughing and crying at the same time.

Ethel May began to tell the story from the beginning, and she was stammering as she laughed and waved her hands in the air. I'll never forget that scene, because it was so unlike her to get so excited. We were having quite a party!

Finally, Kevin said, "Well, Marv, let's walk!" It was getting late, so we took a short walk around the campground, then talked until after midnight about what we should do next. Should we go home Wednesday rather than wait until Saturday as planned? What was going to happen when everyone found out?

The four of us were up early Wednesday morning. We enjoyed breakfast and continued to marvel at what God had done. Kevin and Sandy's daughter, Batina, her husband, Rich (the same Rich who had the vision of the angel), and their daughter were coming to the campground to spend the day. Rich planned to stay with me while the others went to the nearby water park.

As Rich tells it: "The parking lot was full, so we had to park a long distance from the camper. As Batina and I walked, I looked ahead and saw Marvin and Ethel May walking toward us. My first thought was that Ethel May was helping Marvin along. But as we came closer, Marvin was smiling and reaching his arms out to me. I was incredulous, thinking, 'What's different about this picture?'"

Tears streamed down Rich's face as we hugged and laughed and cried. Ethel May and I told them the story on our way back to the campsite. Even though Rich's plans to sit with me for the day had changed to walking with me, we did, indeed, have a wonderful visit while the others played at the water park.

Kevin, Sandy, Ethel May, and I had just finished supper when a van pulled up beside the camper and out jumped Debbie. Keith, laughing and waving from the driver's seat, had dropped her off before proceeding to the parking lot, knowing she could wait no longer. That scene repeated itself as Becky and Sarah arrived, and soon we were all celebrating together: Keith and Debbie and their children, Abby and Andrew; Chet and Becky and their children, Beverly and Cameron; and Eric and Sarah. (Chet and Becky's third child, Allison, and Eric and Sarah's first, Kaden, were born the following year.)

What a party we had that evening! There were as many shouts and squeals from the grown-ups as there were from my grandchildren as they called, "C'mon, Papaw, let's play!" and, "Look, Mommy, Papaw's walking!" As I pushed my beautiful grandchildren in the swings at the camp's playground, I was overwhelmed with thankfulness to God. Other campers shared our joy as they realized the reason for our celebration.

Ethel May and I stood together and waved as our family pulled out of the parking lot long after dark. Kevin called out to us as we strolled back toward the camper, "Marv, don't forget, we have a meeting tomorrow. You'd better get some sleep!"

The meeting on Thursday was at the office of my friend and area minister, Dr. Wayne Paulsen in Granville, Ohio. He would be expecting me to arrive in the wheelchair, as usual, so Kevin and I wondered how he would react when I walked into the office building without help. As it turned out, Wayne was already outside watching for the van, and as he started across the parking lot, I stepped out and walked toward him.

I will never forget the look on his face as he realized what God had done. With tears flowing freely, we stood for several minutes, arms around each other, brother with brother. Of course, we repeated the whole scene as we entered the building and met with others who were there for the meeting. On our way back to the campground, Kevin said, "Y'know, Marv, I think we're in for lots of celebrating during the next few weeks!"

By Friday afternoon, the news was most definitely out! Friends and relatives called, and some came to see for themselves. A men's Bible study group who had met on Thursday evening decided they would come to the campgrounds Friday after work. Steve Wilcoxen, a chiropractor, was part of this group. "Marv, I just returned from a continuing education seminar, and I want to show you something they covered there." He opened the trunk of his car and pulled out some papers.

"Look at this. By all human standards, you shouldn't be walking, Marv." The article stated that muscles atrophy (deteriorate) rapidly if not used. In fact, it said fifty percent of muscle mass can be lost in three to five weeks. I just smiled and shook my head. God is an awesome God!

Another couple, Pamm and Gerald, had stayed Friday night, so Saturday morning, Kevin, Gerald, and I packed up outside while the women secured the inside of the camper. When we finished, Kevin said, "There's one thing we have to do before we leave. Marv, you've walked, but you haven't run. Let's take a jog." I didn't hesitate. Kevin and Gerald caught up with me, and we ran from one end of the campgrounds to the other. I'm sure the people who were having breakfast outside wondered what in the world these three old men were up to!

Mike and Mary had called to ask if we would stop at their house on our way home Saturday. By the time we rolled into their driveway, there was a small crowd of people who were already celebrating. As I stepped out of the van, there was applause, crying, shouting, and praising God. Several stayed at a distance, taking pictures as everyone lined up to give me a hug. When things had settled down a little, someone said, "Well, Marv, let's see you run across the yard!" I took off, and the air filled once again with applause and shouting.

Several times, as another car approached, I started down the road to meet more of my church family. They would stop the car and get out, and the celebration would begin all over again. Finally, we stood in the driveway, arms around each other, some with hands raised toward heaven, and we prayed and sang and worshipped Almighty God.

Eventually, we went inside and sat in Mike and Mary's family room, telling the story over and over as more people came in. Every time someone opened the front door, the whole crowd stood to watch the reaction, the looks on the callers' faces as I walked toward them, and the party would start all over again. This continued until late afternoon, and finally

Ethel May and I drove home, wondering what Sunday morning would bring.

I left the house early Sunday morning to visit Harvestime Church and Fellowship Chapel, churches in Vinton whose pastors are friends of mine. From the time the first symptoms of illness had appeared, people in both churches had been praying for me. One group had even held a twenty-four-hour prayer vigil during which they scheduled someone to actually be in their church building praying for me for hours at a time. This had been almost two years before my healing took place, but, like the people of Vinton Baptist Church, they had continued to pray faithfully.

When I drove into the parking lot of the Fellowship Chapel, Pastor Paul Ring had just parked his car, and within a few minutes he and others who had arrived for Sunday school were celebrating with me. Again, there were tears of joy, hugs, clapping of hands, and praise offered to an awesome God. Paul later told me the excitement continued throughout their worship service. It was the same at Harvestime, and after their service, several members drove to Vinton Baptist to join our extended celebration.

By the time I parked my car and walked to the front door of Vinton Baptist Church, the praise band was playing, and I could hear the singing. Of course, by this time everyone knew about the healing, and the place was jumping with excitement and anticipation of my arrival. The children's church room and the nurseries were empty, because everyone wanted to join the celebration in the sanctuary. A small crowd greeted me at the door, and after many hugs and praises to God, I made my way through the sanctuary doors and down the aisle.

I was blessed with what I call a "wow" moment as I stood in the front row and enjoyed the music and singing of more than four hundred worshipers. The people were still standing when the worship leader called me to the platform, and the applause and praise to God seemed to go on forever. When the noise died down, I said, "I have a wheelchair for sale," and once again the room was filled with joyous praise.

Of course, there was no way I was going to stay put behind the podium. I'm sure the necks of the congregation were well exercised that day as I paced from one end of the platform to the other as I described the week and how God had brought about such a miracle.

The service concluded with the entire congregation gathered around me at the altar for a prayer of thanksgiving and praise. What an awesome God we serve!

> Give thanks to the Lord, call on his name;
> make known among the nations what he has done.
> Sing to him, sing praise to him;
> tell of all his wonderful acts.
> Glory in his holy name;
> let the hearts of those who seek the Lord rejoice.
> —Psalm 105:1–3

CHAPTER NINE

QUITE THE LEARNING EXPERIENCE!

The celebration continued the following Sunday as people packed the sanctuary and praised God with their singing, praying, applause, raising of hands, laughter, tears, and, generally, outward expressions of their love for God and for each other. But the fact is, other than the excitement caused by my continual walking around on the platform and up and down the altar steps (I just couldn't stop!), the worship services didn't change all that much from the way they were before my healing. We continued to celebrate the message of Isaiah 40:28: "Do you not know? Have you not heard? The Lord is the everlasting God, the Creator of the ends of the earth. He will not grow tired or weary, and his understanding no one can fathom." May we never stop celebrating Him!

Since my healing, I often hear, "Pastor Sallee, what did you learn through this experience?" I hardly know where to begin to answer that question.

Wheelchairs are wonderful for increasing the mobility of those who are otherwise unable to move about freely. But let's face it, being confined to a wheelchair is exactly that: confining. I may not understand God's full purpose in all that has happened until I see Him face to face in Heaven, but surely this was a learning experience for me, my family, and for the people of Vinton Baptist Church.

Many times, especially during the second year of the illness, I thought of Job. Of course, I was hoping my story would end like his, with his health and happiness restored. But I also wondered how and why this was happening to me. Had I done something wrong? Was I being punished? Was God trying to teach me something? Was this illness purely physical or was it a "scheme of the devil" against which I should take my stand (Ephesians 6:11)? Not that I have ever been as "blameless and upright before God" as was Job, but I wondered if Satan, as he had done in regard to Job, had spoken to God about Vinton Baptist Church: "Oh, sure, Vinton Baptist Church is growing, and they're planning to build a nice big place where they say they'll serve You. But take Marvin Sallee out of the picture and see what happens. They'll fall apart." Then, maybe God said, "No, they won't fall apart, because they are focused on Me, not on Marvin Sallee. But I will allow this scheme of yours for a time, because it will ultimately accomplish much good."

Was that it, or was it my own pride God was dealing with? During the early years after coming to Vinton, I did, indeed, believe that if something needed to be done, I would have to do it. I had always been a workaholic, anyway, so this kind of thinking only reinforced the addiction. It is painful to admit, but often, rather than delegate a task to someone else, I would forge ahead, thinking someone else should have noticed it needed to be done, anyway, and that I shouldn't have to ask. Besides, I could run circles around everyone else when it came to getting a job done.

Certainly, I should have repented of that pride and asked others to help. I discovered there were many in the congregation who simply needed to be made aware of my needs and the needs of the church. I was also blind to the fact that this was, indeed, a form of pride, which is an idol of the heart that sneaks into the lives of many faithful Christians. Some of us, I've discovered, are very proud of our "humility"!

God made me acutely aware of my pride one day when, because I was too stubborn to ask for help, I had fallen for the tenth time in one morning. As Becky helped me back into the wheelchair, she said, "Dad, don't you know you hurt us when you refuse to ask for help?" I had been telling myself that I didn't want to bother anyone else. But the truth was that, even after so many falls, I just had to prove I could do it myself!

A faithful Christian friend calls this a "ballbat experience." This happens when we're drifting along, thinking we're doing just fine spiritually or that we fully understand a passage of Scripture, and God suddenly opens our eyes as though we've been hit on the head with a ballbat. Thump! Why didn't I see that before? Me? Proud? Yes!

Another "ballbat" hit me just after a doctor told me to get into a wheelchair and stay there. I was sitting in my living room, staring into space, thinking "What does life look like from a wheelchair? How can I preach sitting down? What about weddings and funerals? What about the house and the yard? What about...?" I felt a hand on my shoulder, and Sarah said, "Dad, don't fret."

Suddenly, I realized I was not Super Christian. Not that I had consciously considered myself to be, but the evidence showed otherwise. I had been living as though it was my duty to meet everyone's needs. After all, hadn't I always been the one who fixed things for my family, the go-to guy when someone needed help, the pastor who was always available twenty-four hours a day, seven days a week? Me? Worry? Why, I counseled others not to worry, to trust God! And now my daughter had caught me worrying!

As I mentioned earlier, Debbie once asked me, "Dad, are you afraid?" At that time I wasn't ready to admit it. I didn't want to give in to the fear. But I now realize admitting fear isn't necessarily giving in to it. In fact, before we can have victory over our fears, we must acknowledge they exist. I have learned to say, "Father, I am afraid. Give me the courage to endure whatever comes my way and the strength to honor You in the midst of it." When Jesus said, "Fear not," He obviously knew we would be dealing with fear. With His help, however, we can overcome anything that threatens to control us and shift our focus from trusting in God.

Sometimes overcoming means actively doing something, such as taking swimming lessons to overcome your fear of water, or turning off the TV to overcome the temptation to put off more important tasks. Sometimes it means waiting for God to remove whatever is trying to obstruct our view of Him. Take a look at Peter in Matthew 14, in the account of Jesus walking on the water. Jesus gave him permission to walk on the water, also. Peter had the faith to get out of the boat and start toward Jesus. Then, "when he saw the wind," he gave in to fear and began to sink.

What Peter actually saw, of course, were the *effects* of the wind: boat rocking, water splashing, huge waves of water rising and falling. Perhaps a wave rose up between Jesus and Peter, and rather than remember that Jesus was still just on the other side of that wave, and that the wave was only temporary, Peter shifted his focus, forgot Jesus was there, and gave in to fear.

During the wheelchair experience, I was often tempted to "see the wind": the tremors, the choking, the hassle of getting in and out of the van and through doors, the depression, and so on. But as long as I remembered Jesus was still standing right where He always was, I didn't sink.

Another thing God brought to my attention through the wheelchair experience was Ethel May's unwavering dedication to me and to our marriage. She never complained. On one particularly bad day, after helping me back into the chair after yet another fall, as I apologized for being so much trouble, she put her hand in mine and said, "You know, forty-one years ago I said, 'for better or worse, in sickness and in health.' Honey, I'm going to do whatever it takes to get you through this. We're going to make it!" Not that I had ever doubted our wedding vows, but those words took on a new and deeper meaning for me that day.

I have a much deeper appreciation for friends. I have always thought of the men and women of Vinton Baptist Church as my Christian brothers and sisters, but I don't think I realized the depth of their love for me as their friend. Unlike Job's so-called friends, they didn't put me under a microscope or bring me before a board to answer charges. They trusted (even though they, like the doctors, didn't understand what was going on) that God was in control of the situation.

When I was ready to give up, my church family never wrote me off, never considered asking me to step aside. They were never embarrassed or impatient when a sermon was delayed while I struggled, and there were always cups of water, mints, and cough drops nearby. Someone was always ready to spring into action if I needed anything.

Before the wheelchair experience, I had taken for granted that I would always be able to officiate at weddings and funerals. It is very important to me that these services flow smoothly, without interruptions or awkwardness. As my condition worsened, I became acutely aware that I might never again be able to help with these important times in the lives of my church family. But I was to discover that "smoothly" didn't matter so much to them.

When one young couple asked me to marry them, I advised them they would be much better off to have an associate pastor, since it would surely ruin the ceremony if they tried to work around the wheelchair. But they insisted, and although it was quite an interesting rehearsal, the wedding went well, and they assured me they wouldn't have wanted it any other way. Their encouragement was typical of the love and support I continuously received from so many people.

It was extremely difficult to be where I needed to be (or thought I needed to be) during funerals and the visitations beforehand. Again, my friends stepped up to the plate to help, comforting the families, helping me navigate the cemeteries. Leadership at Vinton Baptist Church extends well beyond the pastors and deacons. Many godly men and women are available whenever there is a need.

These men and women, my brothers and sisters in Christ, mean more to me than I can express. When I came to Vinton twenty-some years ago, one stipulation I gave the church leaders was that the people of the church would help me raise my children. They have kept their word, and we continue as a church family to help each other bring up godly children and grandchildren.

What a journey this life has been so far! Thankfully, God isn't finished with me yet, and I'm still learning and gaining insight into myself, others, and best of all, Him.

I will come and proclaim your mighty acts,
O Sovereign Lord;
I will proclaim your righteousness, yours alone.
Since my youth, O God, you have taught me,
and to this day I declare your marvelous deeds.
Even when I am old and gray, do not forsake me, O God,
till I declare your power to the next generation,
your might to all who are to come.
—Psalm 71:16–18

CHAPTER TEN

ORDINARY CHURCH, EXTRAORDINARY GOD

As I speak at other churches, not only about the healing experience but also about the growth of the ministries of Vinton Baptist Church, I am dismayed by the hopelessness of individuals and congregations. Often their response is, "Well, it's nice that God is doing such great things at your church, but we cannot imagine that happening here." Ten years ago, I did not imagine it at Vinton, either!

God will give us wonderful imaginations if we simply ask. In the book, *My Utmost for His Highest*, Oswald Chambers says, "If you have never used your imagination to put yourself before God, begin to do it now" and, "Imagination is the greatest gift God has given us and it ought to be devoted entirely to Him" (February 11). Since we cannot see God in physical form, we must use our imaginations to picture ourselves in His presence. My worship is greatly enhanced when I close my eyes and imagine myself bowing before Almighty God!

In Colossians 3:2, Paul says, "Set your minds on things above, not on earthly things." The more we study the Bible, the more we take it into our hearts and minds, the better we know the mind of Christ and the more likely we are to be in step with Him on a day-to-day basis. Then we can see this life through His eyes, with His vision.

The vision of who we are to be, both as individuals and as a church body, must come from God. Notice, I said, "who we are to be," not "what we are to do." Before we begin projects and programs that will serve the church and community, we must become people whose hearts and minds are set on knowing God Himself so well that the *doing* comes naturally. Rather than ask God to help us perform some kind of wonderful service, we should first ask Him to give us compassion for others, then show us how we can be used by Him to serve those in need. So often we get this backwards.

As I've discussed in chapter 5, Vinton Baptist Church began to change for the better when the people learned the importance of prayer. James' words, "You do not have because you do not ask God" (James 4:2b), apply to churches with no vision for the future. As we asked (and continue to ask) God to give us direction for the ministries of the church, He gave us a vision of how to serve Him.

Our counseling ministry began this way. Someone noticed the pastor was swamped with appointments for those who desired biblical counseling. In other words, someone recognized a need. After much prayer and discussion, several attended a twelve-week course in biblical counseling, and so that area of ministry has grown.

At the time of this writing, we have several families in the church who are struggling with addictions. Parents, siblings, and friends of those who are in bondage to drugs and alcohol are often at the altar praying desperately for their deliverance. As a result, not only are some in recovery, but God is also directing us toward a more structured ministry of support for those who need help in this area.

Stepping out is what it's all about. In June 2004, God made it clear to me that it was time to leave the wheelchair behind. Actually getting out of it was my choice. I had to consciously decide to take God at His word, get up, and step forward.

For many years Vinton Baptist Church was confined to the "wheelchair" of complacency. We did church well, but we were not a well church. We were stuck in tradition with no vision for the future. When people began to pray in earnest for God's direction for the church, we gradually became aware of our unhealthy state, of our "confinement."

Of course, for a church to be spiritually healthy, the pastor must be spiritually healthy. At some point (most likely as a result of the intentional praying that began in 1992), I had begun to ask God, "Is this all there is?" Church on Sunday morning, Sunday night, Wednesday night, twice-a-year revival meetings. Same ol' same ol'. I had no idea of what God had in mind for the church or for me, so I began to seek Him out. I knew He wanted more than just our treading water. I needed to see a greater vision of a greater purpose for Vinton Baptist Church. I spent many sleepless nights in conversation with God.

Little by little, He began to change me. I had always had a desire to learn and to further my formal education, but as I prayed, I developed an even greater hunger for books on leadership and church growth and development. Of course, much of the information from these books overflowed into Sunday sermons, and soon I was sharing titles with others who were eager to learn, also. I took a stack of books to every deacons' meeting. Often our "book reviews" led to wonderful theological discussions and deeper study of the Bible.

A pastor cannot take the people in a church someplace they don't want to go. As God was giving me instruction and direction, He was also working in the lives of many in the congregation. On Sunday evenings we were more casual than during the morning services, and often we had testimony time. People would stand and tell how God had answered their prayers and how He was working in their lives.

One Sunday evening a man almost jumped to his feet when I asked if there were any testimonies. "I'm reading a great book about a church that grew from a few people to several thousand!" He went on and on about the book, but he couldn't remember the title. He did the same thing the following week, and we laughed when once again he forgot the title. Eventually, we discovered it was *Fresh Wind, Fresh Fire*, by Jim Cymbala, and since this guy was so excited about it, the secretary ordered copies for the church library. Soon more people were excited about this book.

We were encouraged because we knew, even though Vinton was a speck of dust compared to New York City, that God could do the same with our little Baptist church as He did with the Brooklyn Tabernacle. We began to believe we could, indeed, have an impact for God in the Ohio River Valley. In other words, we began to catch the vision.

The word "change" can fill a heart with fear, which leads many Christians, both young and old, to become set in their ways. Some liked things just the way they were and sincerely believed the church could grow without moving away from the old traditions. Now, traditions aren't all bad, but when it comes to the church, we usually stick to them because it is the safe and effortless thing to do. We don't want to step out of the boat, not only because we fear we'll sink but also because we're lazy. Of course, we don't think of it as laziness. We think we're pleasing God by doing church well: begin on time, end on time, follow the schedule printed in the weekly bulletin, and hope and pray nothing happens to disrupt the order of things.

In his book, *The Pursuit of God*, A.W. Tozer says, "To great sections of the Church the art of worship has been lost entirely, and in its place has come that strange and foreign thing called the 'program.'" When our eyes were opened to the fact that it was time to move in a different direction, we asked God to show us how to change. One of the first things He brought to our attention was the bulletin. Why did we have to have a detailed schedule? Now, don't get me wrong. I don't believe for a minute that we shouldn't have a plan for worship. But having it in print seemed to say to those in the pews, "This is the program. This is what is going to happen and when. No interruptions allowed, even by the Holy Spirit."

It was quite unsettling for a few people when they realized the inside front cover of the bulletin would no longer provide them with the security of knowing exactly what was ahead in the Sunday morning service. But over time the people have come to trust the pastors, deacons, worship leaders, and other team leaders to conduct themselves, the worship services, and the business of the various ministries according to God's direction.

Again, prayer is the key.

Sadly, many Christians, even years after turning their lives over to Jesus, remain ignorant of God's character. They may know a little or a lot about what the Bible says, but they haven't "eaten" the message, taken it in as we take in food to help us grow and become healthy. Again, Tozer says, "It is a solemn thing, and no small scandal in the kingdom, to see God's children starving while actually seated at the Father's table" (*The Pursuit of God*). These are the Christians Paul talks about in chapter three of 1 Corinthians, the "mere infants in Christ" (verse 1). There are many "infants" in our churches today who come to church every Sunday to be "fed" after six days of "fasting."

Certainly we should seek out and attend a church where the people truly worship God, where He is the center of their attention and honor. But in regard to "feeding," I must ask, "To be healthy physically, do you eat only once a week?" To be healthy spiritually, we must have a steady diet of the spiritual food God has provided for us in the Bible. If we will take the time to meditate on it, asking Him to open our minds and hearts to the message, we will grow stronger in our faith as we become closer friends with God.

One of the best messages I've read in regard to Bible study is in Buddy Owens' book, *The Way of a Worshiper*. Chapter fifteen, entitled, "Reading God's Mind, Praying God's Thoughts," is full of wonderful advice on how we can get to know God better through meditative Scripture reading.

Church growth that is pleasing to God begins with spiritual growth of the individuals in that church. Christians who truly desire to be more like Jesus in their thinking and behavior must make prayer and meditative Bible study a priority in their lives. I've heard it said, just as you can start a fire by rubbing two sticks together, to set a church on fire for God, we must rub together the two "sticks" of prayer and Bible study.

As members of God's family, we in the church must encourage each other to grow and mature in our step-by-step, day-by-day walk with God. Like many churches today, Vinton Baptist Church is growing rapidly in numbers, which makes it difficult for the pastors to stay in contact with every person who attends services. Small group leaders help us stay connected.

These groups meet throughout the week, some at the church and some in homes, and many people have been greatly helped not only in the area of spiritual growth but also in the area of accountability. This accountability includes helping each other become aware of the "wheelchairs" that are limiting them spiritually. In the next chapter I will discuss some of the things that hinder our spiritual freedom.

I have hidden your word in my heart
that I might not sin against you.
Praise be to you, O Lord;
teach me your decrees.
With my lips I recount
all the laws that come from your mouth.
I rejoice in following your statutes
as one rejoices in great riches.
I meditate on your precepts
and consider your ways.
I delight in your decrees;
I will not neglect your word.
—Psalm 119:11–16

CHAPTER ELEVEN

THE TRUTH WILL SET YOU FREE

There are many good books available that contain more in-depth information and instruction for individuals, counselors, and support groups, and some are listed at the back of this book. However, before we ask God to free us from whatever holds us back spiritually, we must first acknowledge the problem. If we ask, God will help us recognize whatever might be hindering our relationship with Him and with other people in our lives.

So often I've counseled with people who thought their problems would be solved if others would change. How liberating it is to realize we cannot change others! That task belongs only to God. When we get our spiritual eyes focused vertically rather than horizontally and concentrate on being who God wants each of us to be, others will, in God's time, come alongside. Some may not, but our attitude toward them will improve as we learn to see them through His eyes.

Once again, I want to emphasize I am not one of those people who believes it is always God's will that we be healed of physical disabilities or that we are *not* healed because we lack faith. When Jesus said, "Your faith has healed you" (Matthew 9:22; Mark 10:52; Luke 17:19), He was surely referring to faith in *Him*. After all, we can have faith in anything and anyone! Also, in regard to the *amount* of our faith, Jesus said it is not the *how much* but the *Who* (Luke 17:6). Regardless of our physical condition, we can be healthy spiritually, mentally, and emotionally if we will trust Jesus to free us from anything that prevents us from becoming more like Him. The things that stunt our spiritual growth, these "chains of bondage" or "wheelchairs" or whatever we choose to call them, come in many forms. The more obvious are addictions that keep us from living productive, God-honoring lives. But just as confining are anger, resentment, fear, and pride.

The Pharisees who refused to accept Jesus as God were spiritual invalids; they suffered from all the above. Of course, their unbelief separated them from God, but had they been willing, they could have walked away from their confinement. Jesus offered them spiritual freedom, but they chose to stay put, to wallow in their self-righteousness. Christians sometimes do the same.

Jonah's anger and resentment toward the people of Nineveh restrained him and prevented him from enjoying God's blessings. Even though he finally obeyed God, he refused to change his attitude. He was obedient in that he went through the motions of doing what God had instructed him to do, but he clung to his anger and refused to forgive. Aren't we like Jonah sometimes? We feel justified in our anger and harbor resentment toward someone who may have wronged us long ago.

I have talked with people whose lives are obviously affected by deep-seated anger, but they either deny their anger or insist they have the right to feel the way they feel. Remember what God asked Jonah: "Do you have a right to be angry about the vine?" (Jonah 4:9a). God knew Jonah's heart. He knew the real issue wasn't the vine, and He wanted to help Jonah get his priorities in order. However, Jonah wasn't willing to walk away from the idol of his own feelings. He was comfortable in his own self-centered state.

God wants to shift our focus so that we see people and circumstances from *His* perspective. When we learn to see things God's way, we see that Christians, sinners who have been forgiven by God, have no right to withhold forgiveness from others. We must also forgive *ourselves* and leave behind debilitating guilt that has nothing to do with God.

The Bible's account of Jonah ends without revealing whether or not Jonah changed his attitude, but the message is clear. We can confine ourselves to our little shelters of self-absorption where God cannot bless, or we can look to Him for the love and compassion for others that only He can give.

The day after I had officially resigned my position as pastor of the three churches in the Marietta Parish, a lady from one of the churches paid me a visit. "I am upset with you," she said. I thought she was about to say how sorry she was that I was leaving, but she continued, "Six years ago you said something that made me mad, and I have never gotten over it. Do you remember what you said?"

Six years! Of course, I didn't remember, but she reminded me. The offending sentence was one small part of a sermon, and the way she had interpreted the message had caused her much pain. We talked a while, and before she left my study, she had forgiven me. I still shake my head about it.

For six long years this Christian sister had attended church regularly, had gone through the motions of worship and ministry, but an unforgiving spirit had certainly cost her the joy and freedom that comes with keeping in step with God. I know this because, in the following years, whenever we met during my occasional visits to friends, she spoke to me with warmth and kindness, and there was a light in her eyes that hadn't been there before. How sad that she hadn't come to me immediately after that sermon so many years earlier! It had been her choice to stay confined to a "wheelchair" when she could have been free.

Earlier I wrote about my reluctance to face my fears as my physical condition worsened. I had operated under the assumption that I could and would always rise above fear, especially for the sake of my family and the church. However, my denial of my fear only prevented me from turning it over to God so that He could help me deal with it. Like anger, fear itself isn't sinful; how we deal with it will either honor God or dishonor God and lead to more sin.

Who was I to think I might not experience fear in my life? The great prophet, Elijah, even after seeing God's power and being a part of phenomenal miracles, succumbed to fear as he ran from Ahab and Jezebel (1 Kings 18 and 19). For whatever reason he became fearful and ran for his life, his running (and very likely, fatigue) led to his self-imposed isolation and depression. He had quite a pity party as he sat under that tree and asked God to let him die. God, however, got Elijah's attention and brought him back to reality, and He will do the same for us when we allow Him.

Sometimes God's "bringing us back to reality," freeing us from fear and depression, includes seeking professional help, medication, dietary changes, and rest. Whatever the route to recovery, we must never rely on our own emotions, our own feelings. We must continue to believe the truth of God's Word whether we "feel" like it or not. Satan is a crafty enemy and would love for our faith to waver with every change of mood.

The sin of pride may be the sneakiest scheme Satan has in his bag of tricks. I like what Max Lucado says in his book, *He Chose the Nails*: "Pride and shame. You'd never know they are sisters. They appear so different. Pride puffs out her chest. Shame hangs her head. Pride boasts. Shame hides. Pride seeks to be seen. Shame seeks to be avoided.

"But don't be fooled, the emotions have the same parentage. And the emotions have the same impact. They keep you from your Father. . . . If pride is what goes before a fall, then shame is what keeps you from getting up after one." If we cling to our shame and guilt over past mistakes, we discredit God. If He has forgiven us, who are we to refuse to "get over it"?

Sometimes what we think is humility is actually sinful pride. There are people who have been ashamed and depressed about their past for years. Even though they've asked and received God's forgiveness, they continue to wallow in their guilt. What they don't realize is that their feelings of shame have actually become an idol, an object of worship that consumes their thoughts and directs their lives. This behavior keeps us from the Father, from moving forward in our spiritual journey.

You might be wondering, "What exactly do you mean by 'spiritual journey'?" An individual becomes a Christian when he or she believes Jesus is who He says He is and accepts Him not only in "head knowledge" but also in the heart. From that moment on, this person is a member of God's family and will spend eternity in Heaven. What many fail to realize is that the journey has just begun at that point. They seem to think they've arrived, and that's that.

But God has so much more to show us! Forgive the weak comparison, but failing to continue on the journey is like stepping inside the gates of Disney World, looking around in awe, but never going forward to experience everything there is to see and do. When we stop just inside the door, we miss out on the indescribable joy that comes with walking hand in hand with God on a daily basis. Some of the "rides" aren't fun, but God is teaching us and growing us up through each experience.

I am thankful that I no longer need the wheelchair for moving from one place to another, but I am so much more thankful for the ways God continues to release the people of

Vinton Baptist Church (including myself) from anything that keeps us from drawing closer to Him.

> To the Jews who had believed him, Jesus said,
> "If you hold to my teaching, you are really my disciples.
> Then you will know the truth, and the truth will set you free."
> —John 8:31–32

CHAPTER TWELVE

THE GREATEST MIRACLE OF ALL

Ecclesiastes 8:17 says, "then I saw all that God has done. No one can comprehend what goes on under the sun. Despite all his efforts to search it out, man cannot discover its meaning. Even if a wise man claims he knows, he cannot really comprehend it."

I cannot comprehend how the earth was formed or how the planets and stars stay in their places. When I get a glimpse of God's greatness, of His majesty and holiness, I am overwhelmed. Here I am, a tiny speck in the universe, and Almighty God loves me and wants me to know and love Him. As I often say to the congregation at Vinton Baptist Church: *Wow!*

Acts 17:24–27 says, "The God who made the world and everything in it is the Lord of heaven and earth and does not live in temples built by hands. And he is not served by human hands, as if he needed anything, because he himself gives all men life and breath and everything else. From one man he made every nation of men, that they should inhabit the whole earth; and he determined the times set for them and the exact places where they should live. God did this so that men would seek him and perhaps reach out for him and find him, though he is not far from each one of us."

Isn't it amazing that God is actually nearby? And that He wants to save every person on earth from spending eternity in Hell? (See 2 Peter 3:9.) But He leaves the choice to us. Jesus said we are either with Him or against Him (Luke 11:23). He won't force Himself upon us, but He welcomes us with open arms when we turn our lives over to Him. It is a personal decision, not one that can be made by anyone else. It is not a matter of our parents dedicating us as babies or of our confirming our commitment to a church. It is simply telling Jesus we accept His forgiveness for our sins, we believe He is Who He says He is, and that we are ready and willing to turn around and walk in step with Him.

When I was twelve years old, I left my seat in the third pew to kneel at the altar. I talked with God, accepted His forgiveness, and invited Jesus into my heart. Funny thing is, I knew it was a matter of a simple prayer, so I "amened" and stood to return to my seat. But others who had gathered around me continued to pray, so I knelt again, waiting for them to finish. When there was a pause, I stood, but they started again, so back to my knees I went. I guess they thought I needed more praying! (Our church's drama team has reenacted this scene rather comically.)

From that day forward, I have been a member of God's family, His son forever. That I can call God my Father is the greatest miracle of all! I didn't earn the privilege of becoming His son; it was a gift, free for the asking.

What a journey this Christian life has been and continues to be! My favorite of all the great old hymns is "Amazing Grace." The second verse says it well: "Through many dangers, toils and snares, I have already come. 'Tis grace that's brought me safe thus far, and grace will lead me home."

Amen!

Amazing Grace (1779)
by John Newton

Amazing Grace! How sweet the sound
That saved a wretch like me!
I once was lost, but now I'm found.
Was blind, but now I see.

'Twas grace that taught my heart to fear
And grace my fears relieved.
How precious did that grace appear
The hour I first believed.

Thru' many dangers, toils, and snares
I have already come.
'Tis grace that brought me safe thus far,
And grace will lead me home.

When we've been there ten thousand years,
Bright, shining as the sun,
We've no less days to sing God's praise
Than when we first begun.

RECOMMENDED READING

In my personal quest to know God better, I've found studying various translations of the Bible helps me gain a more thorough understanding of His character.

These are some of the books (besides the Bible) that have enhanced the spiritual growth of the people of Vinton Baptist Church. I firmly believe that walking in step with God requires continuous Bible study, prayer and worship, and reading books written by mature, faithful Christians.

Bevere, John, *A Heart Ablaze*. Nashville, TN: Thomas Nelson, 1999.

Blackaby, Henry T., and Claude V. King, *Experiencing God*. Nashville, TN: Broadman/Holman, 1998.

Chambers, Oswald, *My Utmost for His Highest*. Dodd, Mead & Company, 1935.

Cymbala, Jim, *Fresh Wind, Fresh Fire*. Grand Rapids, MI: Zondervan, 1999.

Cymbala, Jim, *Fresh Faith*. Grand Rapids, MI: Zondervan, 1999.

Cymbala, Jim, *Fresh Power*. Grand Rapids, MI: Zondervan, 2001.

Cymbala, Jim, *Breakthrough Prayer*. Grand Rapids, MI: Zondervan, 2003.

Jeremiah, David, *Life Wide Open*. Brentwood, TN: Integrity Publishers, 2003.

Jeremiah, David, *Prayer, the Great Adventure*. Sisters, OR: Multnomah Publishers, Inc., 1999.

London, H. B., Jr., and Neil B. Wiseman, *The Heart of a Great Pastor*. Ventura, CA: Gospel Light, 1999.

Lucado, Max, *He Chose the Nails*. Nashville, TN: Word Publishing, 2002.

Lucado, Max, *He Still Moves Stones*. Nashville, TN: Thomas Nelson, 1999.

Martin, Glen, and Dian Ginter, *Power House*.

Maxwell, John, *The 21 Irrefutable Laws of Leadership*. Nashville, TN: Thomas Nelson, 1998.

Maxwell, John, *Partners in Prayer*. Nashville, TN: 1996.

Maxwell, John, *Developing the Leader Within You*. Nashville, TN: Thomas Nelson, 2001.

Maxwell, John, *Equipping 101*. Nashville, TN: Thomas Nelson, 2003.

McMannis, Erwin Raphael, *Chasing Daylight*. Nashville, TN: Thomas Nelson, 2006.

Minatrea, Milfred, *Shaped by God's Heart*. San Francisco, CA: John Wiley & Sons, 2004.

Ortberg, John, *If You Want To Walk On Water, You've Got To Get Out Of the Boat*. Grand Rapids, MI.: Zondervan, 2001.

Owens, Buddy, *The Way of a Worshiper*. Lake Forest, CA: Purpose Driven Publishing, 2002, 2004, 2005.

Rainer, Thom S., *Breakout Churches*. Grand Rapids, MI: Zondervan, 2004.

Redman, Matt, *The Unquenchable Worshipper*. Ventura, CA: Gospel Light, 2001.

Stanley, Andy, Reggie Joiner, and Lane Jones, *7 Practices of Effective Ministry*. Sisters, OR: Multnomah Publishers, Inc., 2004.

Stanley, Charles, *Handle With Prayer*. Colorado Springs, CO: Cook Communications, 1992.

Swindoll, Charles, Editor, *The Living Insights Study Bible*. Grand Rapids, MI: Zondervan, 1996. (An excellent study Bible which includes articles and comments by Dr. Swindoll. Sadly, it is out of print.)

Tozer, A.W., *The Pursuit of God*. Camp Hill, PA: Christian Publications, Inc., 1993.

Warren, Rick, *The Purpose Driven Church*. Grand Rapids, MI: Zondervan, 1995.

Warren, Rick, *The Purpose Driven Life*. Grand Rapids, MI: Zondervan, 2002.

ENDNOTES

CHAPTER 10 (PAGES 75–80)

1. See Oswald Chambers, *My Utmost for His Highest.*
2. See Jim Cymbala, *Fresh Wind, Fresh Fire.* Grand Rapids, MI: Zondervan, (1999).
3. See A. W. Tozer, *The Pursuit of God.* Camp Hill, PA: Christian Publications, Inc., (1993).
4. Ibid.
5. See Buddy Owens, *The Way of a Worshiper.* Lake Forest, CA: Purpose Driven Publishing, 2002, 2004, 2005.

CHAPTER 11 (PAGE 85)

1. See Max Lucado, *He Chose the Nails.* Nashville, TN: Word Publishing, (2000).